What People

See the People

MW01505016

I highly recommend this book! Bob is a faithful member of Impact Christian Center and serves diligently on our board of directors. Each week, he teaches our adult Sunday school class and consistently demonstrates his deep devotion to Christ.

Bob has a sincere passion for leading others to Jesus and has faithfully worked alongside us in reaching many souls for the Kingdom. His straightforward and practical teaching style will empower you to grow in your walk with Christ and to confidently share His love with those around you.

This book is a valuable resource for anyone desiring to deepen their faith and become more effective in ministry.

Pastor Darrel Douds,
Impact Christian Center of Fort Worth

We've known Bob for years as a great Bible teacher and Vicki as a wonderful prayer warrior. You will see their hearts as Bob teaches clearly and concisely about the importance of simply loving people as Jesus did. He will take you to other lands as he shares nuggets from his travels all over the world. His descriptions are down to earth and interesting, and will make you feel as though you have sat down to talk with him as he urges you to *see* God's wonderful creation of people.

Ken and Becky Dornhecker, Evangelism Fellowship

The book *See the People* by Bob and Vicki Fox is right on in a world needing to hear how the Lord sees the (HIS) People. How the Lord wants to lead in the ever-vanishing peace all seek and want. Bob and Vicki are true warriors spiritually and can be trusted with the WORD. I highly recommend this book to those needing and wanting to go deeper in knowing more how the Lord sees the people ... and how we should see the people as Christ followers.

Dr. Joseph Nawrocki, MD, Rock's Medical Outreach

Bob and Vicki Fox have poured their hearts into *See the People*, a powerful guide that radiates compassion and purpose. With unwavering faith and practical wisdom, they inspire us to see others through God's eyes and act with love to lead them to salvation. This book is a heartfelt call to action, blending personal stories, scriptural truth, and actionable steps that will transform lives. It's a must-read for anyone seeking to make an eternal impact.

Don Williams, Entrepreneur, 9X Author, Advisor

See the People provides timely, step-by-step prayer strategies and witnessing tips to equip believers to share Jesus's genuine love, understanding that each person is deeply cherished by their Creator. Drawing from Robert Fox's extensive world travel in the oil business, exposing him to people of diverse nationalities and cultures, Robert & Vicki have crafted an eye-opening guide for Christians to begin seeing all people through God's compassionate eyes.

Dr. Victorya Rogers, DMin,
Co-Author of **How to Talk About Jesus without Freaking Out**

Bob Fox is a servant leader with a kind heart and unassuming manner. I have come to know Bob and his wife, Vicki, through a global professional organization and can attest that their lives are a living representation of the words and message of their book, *See the People*. Their highly active and engaging faith is evident throughout the book that is interwoven with Bob's illustrative "war stories" from his travels in the oil and gas industry. I heartily recommend Bob and Vicki's book that springs from their own daily walk as they share the imperative for having a personal relationship with Jesus Christ, the importance of developing and maintaining a constant and persistent prayer life, and crucial need for sharing the Good News. This is an excellent and sometimes challenging read for us Christians, as we are reminded and encouraged about our mission as a Church and as believers, as well for non-believers seeking answers and meaning in life.

John Tittle, President of FEI Fort Worth,
Tittle Advisory Group

Bob and Vicki's book, *See the People,* is truly refreshing, inspiring, and informative. It stands out because its primary focus is on what is most important to God's heart: the people for whom Jesus willingly sacrificed His life. This book not only informs but also motivates readers to reflect on their own connections and responsibilities toward others. Their writing is infused with compassion, sincerity, heart, and wisdom. I found the book to be solid in every respect: scripturally, spiritually, culturally, and socially. The teachings provide a clear and thorough pathway to effectively communicate the message of the gospel of Jesus Christ. I was impressed by Bob's understanding of world cultures, especially world religions, and his ability to approach people with different views with humility and love instead of angst or hostility. I've observed that many Western Christians seem unaware, misinformed, or unprepared to share the most compelling and powerful message that God has given us to spread to the entire human race. This book serves as an excellent gateway, guiding us on the right path to fulfilling our mission. Bob and Vicki strike a great balance between biblical revelation and common sense, empowering us to "do our job" well. If you want to be equipped, empowered, and confident to "See the People" and effectively reach others for Christ, I encourage you to read this book and apply the principles you learn.

Todd and Julie Powers, Empower International Ministries

Bob and Vicki Fox are living examples of what it means to follow Jesus Christ. *See the People* will open your eyes to the multitudes in need of a Savior. As an American girl traveling in Germany in 1995, I was saved because total strangers shared the gospel with me, and my whole life changed. Too many Christians are fearful of people who believe differently from them, but Jesus calls the lost sheep to enter the sheepfold. This book will radically alter your perspective and help you see—truly see—the lost people all around you, and call you higher to the gift of evangelism. Share your story. Share your time. Share the gospel—eternity is at stake.

Jennifer Strickland, Founder, URMore.org, Speaker, and Author of Beautiful Lies, Girl Perfect, and I Am a Woman: Taking Back Our Name

SEE †HE PEOPLE

Achieving a Better World—
One Life at a Time

Bob & Vicki Fox

HigherLife Development Services, Inc.
2342 Westminster Terrace, Oviedo, FL 32765
(407) 563-4806, HigherLifePublishing.com

©2025 by Bob Fox, with contributions by Vicki Fox

All rights reserved. No part of this book may be reproduced without written permission from the publisher or copyright holder, nor may any part of this book be transmitted in any form or by any means electronic, mechanical, photocopying, recording, or other, without prior written permission from the publisher or copyright holder.

Unless otherwise noted, Scriptures are taken from the *New King James Version*®. Copyright © 1982 by Thomas Nelson. Used by permission. All rights reserved.

Scripture quotations marked AMPC are taken from the *Classic Edition, Amplified Bible*, Copyright © 1987 by the Lockman Foundation. Used by permission. All rights reserved.

Scripture quotations marked AMP are taken from the *Amplified*® *Bible*, Copyright © 1954, 1958, 1962, 1964, 1965, 1987 by the Lockman Foundation. Used by permission.

Scripture quotations marked NLT are taken from the *Holy Bible, New Living Translation*, copyright © 1996, 2004, 2007 by Tyndale House Foundation. Used by permission of Tyndale House Publishers, Inc., Carol Stream, Illinois 60188. All rights reserved.

Scripture quotations marked NASB are taken from the *Holy Bible: New American Standard Bible*. Copyright © 1995, 2020. LaHabra, CA: The Lockman Foundation. Used by permission. All rights reserved.

Published 2025

Printed in the United States of America

30 29 28 27 26 25   1 2 3 4 5

ISBN: 978-1-964081-42-7 (paperback)
ISBN: 978-1-964081-58-8 (ebook)
Copyright Case Number: 1-14910619493

Contents

Chapter 1

See the People

One rare, bright, and crisp fall day in Texas while sitting in my backyard, the Lord spoke to me, "See the people everywhere you go and wherever you are! All of them have needs. Some need to accept Jesus as their Lord and Savior, some need healing, some need prayer for their families, and I want to meet all their needs."

One of the pleasures of working in the oil and gas industry is that you get to travel off the beaten path of normal tourist destinations. When I applied for my Global Entry card, the interviewer commented jokingly after reviewing my passport, "I see you have been traveling to all the vacation hotspots." She laughed and stamped the approval, sending me off to more adventures.

After 9/11, I was requested to go to Saudi Arabia for the first time. Saudi Arabia is 100 percent Muslim. Speaking with them about another faith is illegal. Since Saudi Arabia at the time was the world's number one producer of oil and gas, it was important to my company that I build good relationships with the Saudis to help grow the business.

Because of 9/11, I tried to get out of it. Normally, I could send someone else but no matter what I tried, I was unable to delegate it.

Before I go on trips, I review the country, customs, climate, recent events, and U.S. State Department website, among other things. Saudi Arabia requires visas for visitors, so I went through the application process hoping the Saudi government would turn me down.

The visa was quickly approved.

I have learned over the years to detect the spiritual forces ruling over a country.

> *For we do not wrestle against flesh and blood, but against principalities, against powers, against the rulers of the darkness of this age, against spiritual hosts of wickedness in the heavenly places.* (Ephesians 6:12)

In the AMPC version, it refers to "[the master spirits who are] the world rulers of this present darkness, against the spirit forces of wickedness in the heavenly (supernatural) sphere."

What does that feel like? In Saudi Arabia, it is an oppressive, violent, non-tolerant atmosphere. Where there is no resistance to a spirit dominating over an area, the government will reflect that spirit. We'll discuss this more in chapter four, "Bind the Enemy Off of Their Minds."

Before traveling, I always check the weather forecast so I know how to pack. Typically, the Middle East is predictable— hot and hotter. One time, the forecast included snow, so I felt dumb packing my heavy leather coat but I am glad I did. On that trip, the wind whipping across the desert would make anyone stay inside for the whole trip, but I had both business and a prayer mission to conduct. As a travel note, I learned to always carry something to brush the sand off of my shoes and clothes each day because, by the end of the trip, I would look like a sand-covered person. My wife, Vicki, would always comment about the sand in the suitcases, pockets, shoes, hair, nails, and other unexpected places.

There are some practices in the Middle East that you always have to be mindful of. First, never show them the bottom of your shoes. This symbolizes domination, which ends discussions quickly. Every time I wanted to cross my legs, I had to stop myself to avoid exposing the bottom of my shoe. Second, never ever ask about their daughters or wives, only about their sons. Why? Because females really do not matter. Third, never converse with a woman. You only converse with the husband or a brother who is with her if for some reason you want to address the woman at all. Once, I was boarding a plane with a friend when a woman covered in all black from head to toe dropped her baby's pacifier. Being a kind gentleman, my friend picked it up and asked whether it was hers. An international incident nearly ensued as the man with her addressed him in Arabic. By the grace of God, they stopped and continued boarding the plane. I took the magic moment to whisper in his ear, "Cannot take you anywhere."

Coming off the plane in Saudi Arabia I could feel the normal heat of the day. The people working in the country told me the temperature gauges only measure up to 120 degrees Fahrenheit, but the temperatures go higher than that on many days. Thank God the customs area was air conditioned. Agents were dressed in their traditional robes and the women in line had the traditional black coverings from head to toe. The women could not look you in the eyes, lest they be accused of flirting with you. A few people in the various lines made some snide remarks and were escorted out of the line into other rooms. I have already learned when traveling you do not make comments or give any gestures that might turn people against you, no matter what country you are in. You do not post things on social media making social comments or derogatory remarks.

While in line, I was conversing with the Lord, remarking what the Lord must think of these people who tend to hate Christians and Jews and wouldn't have a problem killing us if given the chance. It was a quiet, one-sided commentary for a while. Since I asked the Lord for His opinion, He told me: "These are the people that I love and that I died for."

Just like that, I started seeing them like Jesus did—with a heart of compassion. It is amazing how the Lord can make one comment and reset your entire perspective. Not a lot of words are needed.

Normally I try to sleep from the airport to the hotel, but I stayed awake to get a good look at the surroundings. After going through all the military confines, machine guns on military trucks with guard dogs and metal detectors sweeping under our vehicle, we reached my hotel room, a basic bed and bathroom. I asked about staying in public hotels but they said some people had mysteriously died in the night, "so this is the only place you can stay."

I then asked about going for walks in the walled-in courtyard, but they told me that they had random mortars coming in, so they did not advise it. I was limited to the room and the restaurant inside the confines.

See the People

It has improved since then, but at that time, there were zero entertainment opportunities in Saudi Arabia. I had a lot of time on my hands. I had realized by now that the reason I could not get out of the trip was because the Lord wanted someone to pray for the people from inside the country. I got on my knees.

Businesspeople can get into places where ministers cannot. Even the most corrupt countries in the world want to do business. The challenge is to keep the corruption out of your life—an ongoing challenge as the bombardment is continuous and everywhere.

Each night after the business meetings I would return to the room and start praying again, sometimes reading the Scriptures aloud in prayer.

I returned to Middle Eastern countries several times, visiting Saudia Arabia, Bahrain, Oman, Kuwait, and the United Arab Emirates with the same mission—to pray from inside the countries for those nations and the people. I am sure other people were called to the same mission, and I also met several Christians who lived and worked there. Whether Muslims, Hindus, Buddhists, Shintoists, or part of any other religion, they do know how to worship something. They are loved by God and Jesus died for them.

"These are the people that I love and that I died for."

MULTITUDES

As a businessperson, I see a lot of people. I see people weaving in and out of traffic every day, including me, but don't really think much about it unless someone cuts me off. Unless someone steps right in front of me, I'm one of the best at walking in and out of crowds without noticing a single person. When I have to go into a store for something, my goal is to get in and get out as quickly as possible. I do love the theoretically faster self-checkout areas as long as we can find the bar code. (This is why clothing stores put the men's section next to the exits.) I see people constantly and, like most, often seek the solace of my quiet home at the end of the day. However, according to Joel 3:14:

> *Multitudes, multitudes in the valley of decision! For the day of the LORD is near in the valley of decision.*

What does "multitudes" mean? "Multitude" is a general term that simply means a large number, so we need to add some perspective. According to Worldpopulationreview.com, the latest global population estimates for 2022 are as follows:

Total Populations	8.0 Billion
Christianity	2.38 billion
Islam	1.9 billion
Hinduism	1.16 billion
Buddhism	0.5 billion
Shintoism	0.3 billion
Judaism	0.02 billion
Other/No Belief	1.74 billion

See the People

Every day across the world, according to the World Population Review, 166,324 people die. According to that same website, there are 367,594 births per day.

Imagine for a moment that you could sit out in space and watch people leaving through deaths and people arriving through births. The Gospel, which translated into English could be called the "Good News," offers opportunities for those alive on the planet to come into the knowledge of God and the saving knowledge of Jesus Christ. The sobering news is that, once they leave the earth through death, their opportunity to choose no longer exists and they go to their eternal destination.

Jesus saw the same picture of multitudes and commented:

But when He saw the multitudes, He was moved with compassion for them, because they were weary and scattered, like sheep having no shepherd. Then He said to His disciples, "The harvest truly is plentiful, but the laborers are few. Therefore, pray the Lord of the harvest to send out laborers into His harvest." (Matthew 9:36–38)

I shared the numbers above not to discourage but to say—chances are good you know people that have not put their faith in Jesus as their Savior. When I have the chance to speak in front of Christians, I typically challenge them with this: if all your friends and family are saved, then it's time to broaden your circles of influence.

Anyone who is "saved" is a laborer. We all have relationships with people who are not saved. If you belong to any organization with more than a few, there are people around you who are not saved, even in our churches.

A circle of influence is a sphere of people with whom we come into contact and in whom we are willing to invest time and effort to see their lives changed for the good. When we look at the Bible, Jesus (our example) started with the twelve. His circle grew to seventy, and then after the resurrection over five hundred people saw Him at one time (I Corinthians 15:3–8).

PRAYER FOR ALL PEOPLE

When we give money and prayers to a church, evangelist, or any other ministry, they can help reach the lost but they cannot do this by themselves. It requires all of us working together to reach people where they are. Each of us has (or should have) relationships that the churches will not be able to reach without our help.

No matter what country you are in, there are multitudes that need to come to the saving knowledge of Jesus Christ.

As Christians, our goal should be to take as many people to heaven with us as possible.

There are people that we come into relationship with for a season, and then there are those rare lifetime friends. Our first goal is to look around and see the people nearest to us that may need to be persuaded toward the Lord Jesus.

If you are struggling with whether Jesus is the only way, you can skip to chapter two, "Are There Many Roads to Heaven?" Then, come back to this chapter.

When I ask the question of people in church, "How many of you are saved and in church because someone prayed for you?"—typically 100 percent of the people in the room raise their hands. In conversations, I ask who that person was, and usually they have a specific name but they also add that there were many others who prayed for them and will remain unknown until heaven. I can say the same.

Then they often say something like, "That person wore the carpet out praying for me." To "wear the carpet out" is to be persistent in prayer. It is amazing the power of prayers when we persist in them until the answer comes!

"Each of us has (or should have) relationships that the churches will not be able to reach without our help."

God is not holding out on certain people. According to I Timothy 2:1–4:

> *Therefore I exhort first of all that supplications, prayers, intercessions, and giving of thanks be made for all men [people], for kings and all who are in authority, that we may lead a quiet and peaceable life in all godliness and reverence. For this is good and acceptable in the sight of God our Savior, who desires all men to be saved and to come to the knowledge of the truth.*

"All men" means all mankind; that is, all people.

Scriptures are not just random sayings of different topics. They are interwoven and there are themes. There is a connection between praying for all people and praying "for kings and all who are in authority." The outcome of those prayers is "a quiet and peaceable life in all godliness and reverence." Because

God desires that all are saved "and come to the knowledge of the truth," when we pray for others our desires line up with His. In the end, isn't that the point?

My number one desire for every person I meet is that they live with peace in their heart and mind, and extend peace to the people around them.

All humans are eternal beings, meaning you will never just cease to exist. Each will eventually pass from this life to the next depending upon the savior they selected. Since it is an eternal destination, we want to give them every opportunity to select Jesus as their Lord and Savior.

What does "all people" mean?

When I teach or engage in conversations, I often have to stop and define terms just to make sure we are speaking the same language and are on the same page. For example, how do we identify the God about whom we are speaking? And how is eternal or everlasting life defined?

He who does not love does not know God, for God is love. (I John 4:8)

Here, God defines Himself as love. This is not the kind of love we are used to. People may throw in the towel on loving you for any number of reasons: offenses, hurts, misunderstandings. God's love is often referred to as never-ending, everlasting, and unconditional love, meaning He never stops loving no matter what.

"My number one desire for every person I meet is that they live with peace in their heart and mind, and extend peace to the people around them."

A Scripture that often shows up at sporting and other public events is John 3:16, where Jesus said:

For God so loved the world that He gave His only begotten Son, that whoever believes in Him should not perish but have everlasting life.

"The world" is defined as everyone who is not saved. That means, numerically, only about 30 percent of the 8 billion people on planet Earth would go to heaven if Jesus chose to return today.

Eternal life means an ongoing relationship with God. Christianity is a relationship-oriented faith where you have access to the Father and the Son through what Jesus did for us in His death, burial, and resurrection. Jesus said:

And this is eternal life, that they may know You, the only true God, and Jesus Christ whom You have sent. (John 17:3)

The word "know" refers to an intimate love. He is not interested in a drive-by relationship but wants us to know Him personally. It is always great to remember that He wants an intimate relationship with us for all eternity—starting now.

People often ask, "What is God's perfect will concerning (name the subject)?"

God desires that all people be saved. It is mind-boggling, but God desires to have a relationship with every person that accepts the sacrifice of His Son. He knows what I am going to say before I say it. He knows what I need even before I ask.

What I like about the Good News is that God spells it out through many different situations and life circumstances, from prostitutes to eunuchs to a little old lady who drops her last coin into an offering while wealthy religious leaders scoff at her. He shows us all these scenarios so that people like me do not mess it up. God is super loving. He understands that we need Him to keep it simple for us.

God spells out through Scripture what He will agree with me when I pray. If God says something is His desire and I pray according to that desire consistently and with perseverance, then I should expect that prayer to come to pass.

> *Now this is the confidence that we have in Him, that if we ask anything according to His will, He hears us. And if we know that He hears us, whatever we ask, we know that we have the petitions that we have asked of Him.*
> (I John 5:14–15)

When He says His desire is for all people to be saved, then that means every living person on the earth today is qualified for this regardless of the life they have led thus far.

FREE WILL

Our Creator gave three gifts to all people: free will, eternity, and the path.

See the People

God gave each person a free will to decide their own destiny. That includes the ability to choose whether to follow Him or not. I am thankful that God did not create billions of robotic people that have no choice in what they do with their life. Some people believe in predestination, but predestination in the Bible is referring to following God's plan or will for our life. You have to get saved first; then you can qualify to know God's plan for your life.

In several passages, God tells His people to choose.

I call heaven and earth as witnesses today against you, that I have set before you life and death, blessing and cursing; therefore, choose life, that both you and your descendants may live. (Deuteronomy 30:19)

Once the bondage of sin was broken by the death, burial, and resurrection of Jesus, the power of choice was restored to humanity. God is so loving that He gives us a choice but then spells out the right one. He never forces Himself on anyone.

Most people I have met would explain their life as a journey searching for meaning, searching for things that make us feel good, even searching the gods of other religions. Thank God someone was praying for me. After hearing the Good News preached several times, my life was dramatically changed. I was one of those people that probably had smoke coming off my backside when I finally gave my life to the Lord. It seemed like everywhere I turned people were coming to me to talk about the Lord.

People ask how God can be so loving and still send people to hell. Actually, people have the free will to choose their own eternal destination.

In whatever you judge another you condemn yourself.
(Romans 2:1)

Judge not, and you shall not be judged. Condemn not, and you shall not be condemned. Forgive, and you will be forgiven. (Luke 6:37)

There is therefore now no condemnation to those who are in Christ Jesus, who do not walk according to the flesh, but according to the Spirit. For the law of the Spirit of life in Christ Jesus has made me free from the law of sin and death. (Romans 8:1–2)

In Christ, salvation is no longer a matter of keeping the ten commandments or any other religious law. The only question the Father asks is: Did you accept the sacrifice My Son made in His death, burial, and resurrection? That is the key question for everyone on earth.

ETERNITY

The second gift He gave to each person is eternity.

He has made everything beautiful in its time. Also He has put eternity in their hearts, except that no one can find out the work that God does from beginning to end. (Ecclesiastes 3:11)

The Amplified Bible says it this way:

He has made everything beautiful and appropriate in its time. He has also planted eternity [a sense of divine purpose] in the human heart [a mysterious longing which nothing under the sun can satisfy, except God].

God placed eternity in our hearts where He has also put a sense of divine purpose. It does not matter where you go on planet Earth— people intuitively know there is something bigger than themselves. They even mention things like a "higher power" in their discussions. Many times, this leads to them worship something. People bow to statues, nature, sports, and stars. They worship geographical locations such as Mecca, celebrities, animals, and even dead people. The New Testament answer to that is John 1:9:

There it was—the true Light [was then] coming into the world [the genuine, perfect, steadfast Light] that illumines every person. (AMPC)

Everyone coming into the world has eternity or the true light implanted in their heart, meaning everyone has a God consciousness on the inside of them. Even the unexplored territories of the world have identified someone or something to worship.

In response to the popular objections, "What about people that have never heard the Good News?" or, "What happens to people who thought that what they believed was true?" Romans 1:20 says:

For ever since the world was created, people have seen the earth and sky. Through everything God made, they can clearly see his invisible qualities—his eternal power and divine nature. So they have no excuse for not knowing God. (NLT)

When people look at creation, they can't help but conclude a divine maker. When people look at the skies or animals or nature around them, the first thing that comes to them is that someone had to have created this. They know there is something bigger out there. Most people don't go down the road of a few "elite" thinkers who propose that colossal messes came together to create order.

"Everyone has a God consciousness on the inside of them."

THE PATH

The third gift God gave to each person is the path to eternal salvation spelled out in the death, burial, and resurrection of Jesus.

This gets spelled out over and over in the Scriptures with phrases like:

- "[For] all men to be saved and to come to the knowledge of the truth" (I Tim. 2:4).
- "He died to sin once for all" (Rom. 6:10).
- "He did once for all when He offered up Himself" (Heb. 7:27).
- "He entered the Most Holy Place once for all" (Heb. 9:12). "That [none] should perish but that all should come to repentance" (II Pet. 3:9).
- "No other name under heaven . . . by which we must be saved" (Acts 4:12).

All are eligible for salvation.

"All" should always mean "all." I have heard of people digging into the word "all" in different languages, and the summation of all that intellectual digging and rationalizing is that "all" still means "all." Every person is eligible. Regardless of what they have done with their life thus far, anyone can receive salvation—even your worst cousin, the most wicked government official, the meanest boss, the most annoying church member, the most violent criminal, the sickest mass murderer, the rapist, the abusive spouse, the atheist who has cursed God, and even me. Every person still breathing is eligible. Our God is so amazingly merciful and gracious.

> For if we sin willfully after we have received the knowledge of the truth, there no longer remains a sacrifice for sins, but a certain fearful expectation of judgment, and fiery indignation which will devour the adversaries. (Hebrews 10:26-27)

If all are eligible to receive salvation, then why are not all saved? Because each person must decide for themselves. I cannot ride the coattails of anyone else—not my spouse, children, parents, or other relatives. Even if I was a fourth-generation preacher, which I am not, that doesn't get me in either.

Jesus made the way, and each person has the ability to choose.

You can impact other people's lives through your prayers, words, and actions around them. In case you are pondering that the person you have in mind has gone too far, or worshiped too many idols, or cursed God, or other horrible things, let these Scriptures inform your understanding.

God our Savior desires all people to be saved and come to the knowledge of the truth.

*I urge you, first of all, to pray for all people. Ask God to help them; intercede on their behalf, and give thanks for them. Pray this way for kings and all who are in authority so that we can live peaceful and quiet lives marked by godliness and dignity. This is good and pleases God **our Savior, who wants everyone to be saved and to understand the truth.** For, there is one God and one Mediator who can reconcile God and humanity—the man Christ Jesus. He gave his life to purchase freedom for everyone. This is the message God gave to the world at just the right time.* (I Timothy 2:1–6 NLT, emphasis mine)

He died once for all.

*Knowing that Christ, having been raised from the dead, dies no more. Death no longer has dominion over Him. **For the death that He died, He died to sin once for all;** but the life that He lives, He lives to God.* (Romans 6:9–10, emphasis mine)

He did it once for all.

*Who does not need daily, as those high priests, to offer up sacrifices, first for His own sins and then for the people's, **for this He did once for all when He offered up Himself.*** (Hebrews 7:27, emphasis mine)

See the People

He entered the Most Holy Place once for all.

*But Christ came as High Priest of the good things to come, with the greater and more perfect tabernacle not made with hands, that is, not of this creation. Not with the blood of goats and calves, **but with His own blood He entered the Most Holy Place once for all, having obtained eternal redemption.*** (Hebrews 9:11–12, emphasis mine)

He is not willing that any should perish.

*But, beloved, do not forget this one thing, that with the Lord one day is as a thousand years, and a thousand years as one day. **The Lord is not slack concerning His promise, as some count slackness, but is longsuffering toward us, not willing that any should perish but that all should come to repentance.*** (II Peter 3:8–9, emphasis mine)

There is no other name under heaven by which we must be saved.

*"Let it be known to you all, and to all the people of Israel, that by the name of Jesus Christ of Nazareth, whom you crucified, whom God raised from the dead, by Him this man stands here before you whole. This is the 'stone which was rejected by you builders, which has become the chief cornerstone.' **Nor is there salvation in any other, for there is no other name under heaven given among men by which we must be saved." Now***

when they saw the boldness of Peter and John, and perceived that they were uneducated and untrained men, they marveled. And they realized that they had been with Jesus. (Acts 4:10–13, emphasis mine)

The blood Jesus shed was more than enough.

*For it pleased the Father that in Him all the fullness should dwell, and by Him to reconcile all things to Himself, by Him, whether things on earth or things in heaven, **having made peace through the blood of His cross.*** (Colossians 1:19–20, emphasis mine)

The price has been paid for us to have intimate fellowship with God so that we may walk as He walked in our full purpose for God—but we have to accept it to walk in it.

So, how can we say the most wicked person in the world can accept Jesus as their Lord and Savior and live a life of blessing? The blood of Jesus was more than enough to pay for every sin.

Atheists run into the blood of Jesus, seeing things they cannot logic away. Dreams and visions come to people who once preached that the Good News is illegal. We can preach, talk, minister, and hope but we cannot accept Jesus for them. This is where their free will comes into play. They must come to Him themselves, but we can impact anyone from individuals to the nations. We can engage people wherever they are. Jesus delegated the authority to us to bring in the harvest of souls. He will work with us to confirm His Word with signs following.

*And then he told them, "Go into all the world and preach
the Good News to everyone. Anyone who believes and is
baptized will be saved. But anyone who refuses to believe will be condemned. These miraculous signs will ac-
company those who believe."* (Mark 16:15–17 NLT)

WISDOM FROM VICKI

Vicki is a deluxe prayer warrior and enjoys leading people
to the Lord. We each took the StrengthFinders survey spon-
sored by Gallup, which highlights your signature strengths.
Vicki's number one strength is harmony, defined as people
who look for consensus. They do not enjoy conflict but are
naturally compelled to seek areas of agreement.

I watch her as she skillfully seeks to find common ground,
looking for areas of agreement but then zoning in on their
spiritual life. I am often amazed at how she causes people to
reconsider their spiritual direction. She finds ways to bring
the Lord into conversations with questions as simple as,
"Where do you go to church?"

When I hear people stuttering in their response, I know
she is going to relate it to current events and tell them something like, "Jesus said He would return during times like this.
I would not want you to get left out."

In this section going forward, we will be hearing from
Vicki so she can share her successes, experiences, and wisdom with us and enrich our process.

Chapter 2

Are There
Many Roads to Heaven?

During my travels to various places throughout the world, I became acquainted with the people's religions and religious beliefs. This was not only a matter of interest but also of necessity as laws and business dealings in any culture are largely dictated by what the people believe. To do a good job, it behooves me to understand how they think and operate. In this chapter, we will first clarify what Jesus actually said about Himself. Then, we'll overview what the five top religions believe and practice.

It is a nice and socially acceptable thought that all paths lead to heaven. It makes us sound intelligent and accepting when conversing with others about the inclusiveness of a god of many names. Being trained as part of the collegiate debate team, I know that it sounds impressive to others when one can argue both sides of any topic. For me, arguing both sides always brought confusion. Your mind typically wants you to decide on what is true. It is one thing to discuss theories and another to talk truth. Truth never changes.

As we journey through life, we all try to determine what is real and absolute truth—the reality that never changes. In the age of AI, we now have to consider whether something really happened or if the "evidence" we are seeing is fake.

Even back in Roman times, a governor by the name of Pontius Pilate asked the question, "What is truth?" (John 18:38). Why did he ask that? Because the Roman government, like many others, started moving away from their foundational principles. To get ahead, they had to adopt the values of the ruling power, which, at that time, was the emperor. What if the emperor was debased and crazy? As the Roman Empire aged, it produced seemingly crazier emperors exhibiting the sin and insanity of practices such as incest, among others. Later, the military generals started taking control, which probably made things worse.

"Was Jesus delusional? A liar? Since Jesus in His own words claimed to be more than a good person or a prophet, when it comes to Him, we must decide whether He is who He said He is."

Dictionary.com defines "truth" as "the true or actual state of a matter; conformity with fact or reality; actuality or actual existence."[1] People claim that the truth is "all roads lead to heaven." How can that be? The roads they are talking about have radically different views on the value of life, people, and even animals. Other beliefs do not line up with what Jesus or the Bible says about truth. People who tout that "all roads lead to heaven" also say things like, "Jesus was just a good person," or, "Jesus was a prophet." Islam claims that Jesus was a prophet while the other religions claim nothing about Jesus at all. Jesus Himself claimed to be much more than just a good person or a prophet.

> *And God said to Moses, "I AM WHO I AM." And He said, "Thus you shall say to the children of Israel, 'I AM has sent me to you.'"* (Exodus 3:14)

> *Jesus said to them, "Most assuredly, I say to you, before Abraham was, I AM."* (John 8:58)

Was Jesus delusional? A liar? Since Jesus in His own words claimed to be more than a good person or a prophet, when it comes to Him, we must decide whether He is who He said He is.

"Ethics" refers to moral principles that govern a person's behavior or the conducting of an activity. Today, ethics is being defined as a personal truth—meaning that what is true for you may not be true for me. If all roads lead to heaven, and personal truth should prevail over biblical truth, then you would think that wherever there is adherence to this belief everyone should just get along, or "co-exist." But these roads and beliefs are vastly different. We run into issues when those

---

1   Dictionary.com, s.v. "Truth," accessed April 4, 2025. https://www.dictionary.com/browse/truth

"truths" collide. God chose one "way" and He spelled out that way for us. Here are a few uncomfortable questions.

- Why are Christians being killed in Africa for their faith, mostly by Muslims?
- Why are Christians being killed in India by the Hindu population?
- Why is the preaching of the Good News about Jesus absolutely prohibited in China?
- Why is Christianity increasingly being classified as hate speech in Europe?
- Why are Buddhists killing Christians in Sri Lanka, Bangladesh, Myanmar, and other Asian countries?

I could go on with country after country. This is easily researchable.

When you are looking for foundational principles to guide your life, there are different paths you can take. Each has its own implications and outcomes. Many people that I have spoken to echo my own beliefs that religion does not lead to life but instead imposes a great deal of pressure on the practitioner to perform by displaying external standards according to religious rules. Isn't Christianity a religion that operates in the same manner? No. Christianity is about the Holy Spirit inside each person leading and guiding them. Rather than working hard to impose external rules and regulations onto the person, the Spirit lives within the Christian causing the Christian to love and agree with God's will and, in that way, live righteously. Jesus said:

I am the way, the truth, and the life. No one comes to the Father except through Me. (John 14:6)

Are There Many Roads to Heaven?

When someone is telling us this is THE way, truth, and life, He is saying that's it. There is there no other way. He is telling us that, to achieve the highest point of living, we need to follow Him—His principles and the path that He laid out.

We will outline several claims Jesus made in the New Testament.

Jesus claimed to be God in the flesh.

Philip said to Him, "Lord, show us the Father, and it is sufficient for us." Jesus said to him, "Have I been with you so long, and yet you have not known Me, Philip? He who has seen Me has seen the Father; so how can you say, 'Show us the Father'? Do you not believe that I am in the Father, and the Father in Me? The words that I speak to you I do not speak on My own authority; but the Father who dwells in Me does the works." (John 14:8–10)

Jesus claimed to be the actual Son of God in power.

As soon as it was day, the elders of the people, both chief priests and scribes, came together and led Him into their council, saying, "If You are the Christ, tell us." But He [Jesus] said to them, "If I tell you, you will by no means believe. And if I also ask you, you will by no means answer Me or let Me go. Hereafter the Son of Man will sit on the right hand of the power of God." Then they all said, "Are You then the Son of God?" So He said to them, "You rightly say that I am." And they said, "What further testimony do we need? For we have heard it ourselves from His own mouth." (Luke 22:66–71)

Jesus claimed that the only way to the Father is through Him.

Thomas said to Him, "Lord, we do not know where You are going, and how can we know the way?" Jesus said to him, "I am the way, the truth, and the life. No one comes to the Father except through Me." (John 14:5–6)

Jesus claimed to be the only source of eternal life.

And this is eternal life, that they may know You, the only true God, and Jesus Christ whom You have sent. (John 17:3)

Jesus claimed that He is now seated at the right hand of the Father.

Again the high priest asked Him, saying to Him, "Are You the Christ, the Son of the Blessed?" Jesus said, "I am. And you will see the Son of Man sitting at the right hand of the Power, and coming with the clouds of heaven." (Mark 14:61–62)

Are There Many Roads to Heaven?

Jesus claimed that in order to experience eternal life with Him and the Father, we have to believe in Him—that He is God.

And as Moses lifted up the serpent in the wilderness, even so must the Son of Man be lifted up, that whoever believes in Him should not perish but have eternal life. For God so loved the world that He gave His only begotten Son, that whoever believes in Him should not perish but have everlasting life. For God did not send His Son into the world to condemn the world, but that the world through Him might be saved. He who believes in Him is not condemned; but he who does not believe is condemned already, because he has not believed in the name of the only begotten Son of God. (John 3:14–18)

Jesus claimed to be the only door or "gate" to enter through for salvation.

So he explained it to them: "I tell you the truth, I am the gate for the sheep. All who came before me were thieves and robbers. But the true sheep did not listen to them. Yes, I am the gate. Those who come in through me will be saved." (John 10:7–9 NLT)

Jesus claimed to be the Christ (the Anointed One).

"The Spirit of the Lord is upon Me, because He has anointed Me to preach the gospel to the poor; He has sent Me to heal the brokenhearted, to proclaim liberty to the captives and recovery of sight to the blind, to set

at liberty those who are oppressed; to proclaim the acceptable year of the Lord." Then He closed the book, and gave it back to the attendant and sat down. And the eyes of all who were in the synagogue were fixed on Him. And He began to say to them, "Today this Scripture is fulfilled in your hearing." (Luke 4:18–21)

Jesus claimed to be the Christ (the Anointed One) and the Son of God.

Then he asked them, "But who do you say I am?" Simon Peter answered, "You are the Messiah, the Son of the living God." Jesus replied, "You are blessed, Simon son of John, because my Father in heaven has revealed this to you. You did not learn this from any human being." (Matthew 16:15–17 NLT)

Why do you think they tried to throw Him over the cliff after making that statement in Luke 4:18–21? Because He was claiming to be the one sent by God to redeem and restore people.

When someone repeatedly makes the claim that they are vital to your life, it begs the question—are they really who they say they are? All who are saved have had to come to grips with these and other statements Jesus made. Through close examination of the picture of reality painted for us by Christ Himself, we can begin to comprehend and accept how loving, gracious, and majestic God is that He would send His only Son to pay the price for us and simplify the decision we all need to make.

FULFILLED PROPHECY

In its basic sense, a prophecy is a prediction. There were also Old Testament prophesies that came true in Jesus and in His life. Jesus is in every book of the Old Testament. One scholar, Dr. J. Barton Payne, in the Encyclopedia of Biblical Prophecy, has found as many as 574 verses in the Old Testament that somehow point to, describe, or reference the coming Messiah, and all except for those claiming His second return have already been fulfilled.

> Now all **this took place to fulfill what was spoken** by the Lord through the prophet. (Matthew 1:22 NASB, emphasis mine)

There are many instances in the New Testament of a phrase such as, "This took place to fulfill" Scripture or prophecy. Using this phrase, the writers of Scripture documented many fulfilled prophecies.

According to Deuteronomy 18:21–22, 100 percent accuracy was required for biblical prophecies regarding the Lord:

> But you may wonder, "How will we know whether or not a prophecy is from the Lord?" If the prophet speaks in the LORD's name but his prediction does not happen or come true, you will know that the LORD did not give that message. That prophet has spoken without my authority and need not be feared. (NLT)

The Lord also said in Jeremiah 28:9:

> So a prophet who predicts peace must show he is right. Only when his predictions come true can we know that he is really from the LORD. (NLT)

In Scripture, you know the speaker is a true prophet of the Lord when what they say comes true.

THE ONLY WAY

Through what He said and did, Jesus laid claim to being the only way to heaven. He said this on multiple occasions throughout the Gospels (the four accounts of the Good News), but for brevity, I only listed one set of Scriptures for each major claim.

You might ask, "Why would I have to deal with His statements? I believe He was a good man who did some good works, but I also believe He was a lot like us and had a sin problem." The challenge is this—if He is who He says with those statements outlined above, then believing otherwise could put you in danger of spending eternity away from Him, outside of heaven—*somewhere* else.

"Through what He said and did, Jesus laid claim to being the only way to heaven."

In this area, we are making decisions that determine our eternal destinies. You do not get a do-over once you pass from this life to the next. There is no such thing as purgatory, reincarnation, or doing enough good works to get to heaven.

It is appointed for men to die once, but after this the judgment. (Hebrews 9:27)

Are There Many Roads to Heaven?

No other system of beliefs offers a relationship with the Father or whatever they call their god. Even the holiest of imams in the Islam religion will tell you they never know whether they have ever done enough to go to their paradise. But we have a merciful God who has told us what we must do to be saved. He spelled it out for us.

Every person has the free will to choose their eternal destiny here and choose where they will spend eternity. God, when He created people, made them that way because He wanted them to choose Him. He did not force the issue but made the way for all people to believe in His only begotten Son. This is the prerequisite to eternal life.

There are two spirits in the world—Christ and antichrist.

Who is a liar but he who denies that Jesus is the Christ? He is antichrist who denies the Father and the Son. (I John 2:22)

And every spirit that does not confess that Jesus Christ has come in the flesh is not of God. And this is the spirit of the Antichrist, which you have heard was coming, and is now already in the world. (I John 4:3)

None of the religions I'll cover here confess Jesus as the Son of God in the flesh, nor do they acknowledge the Father who sent the Son, so they fall into the category of antichrist. If they don't turn to the truth, then their eternal destination is not good.

If you are speaking with someone who is pondering the different path theory, here are some core beliefs to discuss with them. Choose wisely for yourself and help others choose wisely by first praying for them, and then speaking with them about the Lord.

PRIMER ON ISLAM

Islam, which comprises 24 percent of the world's population, means "surrender" or "submission." Islam was founded six hundred years after the life and death of Jesus—a more recent entry into the religions of the world. Mecca, located in Saudi Arabia, is considered by Muslims to be their holiest city. It is important for Muslims to know where Mecca is in relation to their location at any given time so that they can bow and chant specific prayers towards Mecca five times a day. No matter where they are in the world, they must bow and pray in the correct direction. I have literally tripped over people who were bowing and praying on airplanes or in bathrooms because I was not expecting people to be down there on the floor.

Founded six hundred years after the life of Jesus, some of Islam's principles sound almost Christian but are not the same. Their principal document in the Quran (also "Koran") provides some great principles but the fruit of the religion is not love at all.

There are twelve principles of Islam that sound good on the surface but they are only applicable to Muslims and not to infidels. Islam was founded by Muhammad, who became a prophet based on tormenting visions in caves that he wrote down. Tormenting dreams and visions typically come from the demonic realm. Today, the record of those visions is known as the Quran.

Islam is a works-based religion. The people believe that their god, Allah, must be pleased with them for admission into paradise. You can get there if you do enough righteous acts in accordance with the Koran. A "righteous" person actively engages with the community, seeks Islamic knowledge, and is dedicated to guiding others on "the straight path." They practice patience in obedience, resist temptation, and commit to both obligatory and optional acts of worship. This sounds okay, but there is a lot of pressure on the citizens who live under Islam because it is easy to mess up. If you fall off the wagon, there is no repentance. The only recourse is to return to the Islamic practices you were supposed to be doing. There is no way for a practitioner to change from the inside like Christians do through the Holy Spirit.

Muslims observe five pillars:

1. Profession of faith.
2. Pray towards Mecca five times daily.
3. Give alms to the poor and needy.
4. Fast during the month of Ramadan.
5. Undertake a pilgrimage to Mecca.

Today, their guidance comes from imams who issue *fatwas*, which are holy orders or decrees. The *fatwas* can cover every part of life. There are several sects that have differing beliefs, so you can easily wind up with conflicting directions.

Islam's heaven is referred to as *Jannah*, where the good and faithful Muslims go after judgment day. Even the holiest of imams don't really know whether they have done enough good to get into *Jannah*.

"There is a lot of pressure on the citizens who live under Islam because it is easy to mess up. If you fall off the wagon, there is no repentance."

In the Middle East, monarchies predominantly get passed down through family lines. The king of Saudi Arabia (the House of Saud) has absolute power. The king is also custodian of the two holy mosques, and occasionally he uses the title "Defender of Islam." Occasionally, Saudi Arabia will get irritated with another Islamic country for demonstrating un-Islamic behaviors and camp their military on the border or invade to restore Islamic order. Muslims trace their lineage back to Ishmael, the son of Abraham and Hagar.

> *And the Angel of the Lord said to her [Hagar]: "Behold, you are with child, and you shall bear a son. You shall call his name Ishmael, because the Lord has heard your affliction. He shall be a wild man; his hand shall be against every man, and every man's hand against him. And he shall dwell in the presence of all his brethren.* (Genesis 16:11–12)

The Bible describes Ishmael. They use prayer beads as a reminder to pray and to guide them through various prayers. During my meetings with Muslims, some would mutter prayers to cover them for being with me, an infidel according to their book. Infidels are non-believers in Islam. In their book, they have the right not to abide by their agreements with me. Also, they have a right to kill an infidel should the infidel choose not to convert. This is why you see them kill Christians and Jews without a second thought.

There are seventy-three sects in Islam with the Sunni branch being the largest, to which the king's family in Saudi Arabia belongs.

Muslims project the image that they are a united front, but if you are from a different tribe (sect), then they could come against you for not being religious enough. Supposedly, that was what ISIS was all about—everyone they killed was not holy or Muslim enough.

They firmly believe in the patriarchy. Most of them practice Sharia law.

In their belief system, Jesus was a prophet. The reason we started out this chapter citing what Jesus actually said about Himself is because, according to Christ Himself, He was much more than prophet.

If you are speaking with a Muslim where it is not illegal, you can ask if they have any prayer needs that they are not getting answered from Allah. They love to see miracles and our God loves to demonstrate His love for them by making sure the miracle happens. Just pray for them and watch God do what they can't explain.

Today, we are seeing the Lord Jesus appear to many Muslims through dreams and visions. In an online Faithwire article dated June 6, 2023, missionaries reported conversions from Islam to Jesus through dreams. In February 2024, it was reported in Iran that many women were coming to Jesus because so many were praying for them. Our prayers give the Lord the ability to intervene in people's lives and show them the truth. Some recent converts say they had begun to wonder whether Allah was real and asked, "If You're out there, show me." Jesus can appear to them because they asked for the real God to show up. Your prayers for others whom the Lord has placed on your heart never go unanswered.

PRIMER ON HINDUISM

Hinduism, which comprises 14 percent of the world's population, claims to be the oldest living religion, but it's not. The Jewish people were here first, and then Christianity was built on the Jewish foundation.

There are nine beliefs in Hinduism:

1. Believe in one all-pervasive "supreme being" who is both immanent and transcendent, both creator and unmanifest reality.
2. Believe in the divinity of the Four Vedas.
3. Believe that the universe undergoes endless cycles of creation, preservation, and dissolution.
4. Believe in karma, the law of cause and effect by which each individual creates his own destiny through his thoughts, words, and deeds.
5. Believe that the soul reincarnates, evolving through many births until all karmas have been resolved.
6. Believe that divine beings exist in unseen worlds and that temple worship, rituals, sacraments, and personal devotionals create a communion with these devas and gods.
7. Believe that an enlightened master, or satguru, is essential to know the "Transcendent Absolute."
8. Believe that all life is sacred, to be loved and revered, and therefore practice ahimsa, meaning non-injury, in thought, word, and deed.

9. Believe that no religion teaches the only way to salvation above all others, but that all genuine paths are facets of God's light, deserving tolerance and understanding.

Belief number nine is where the thought that "many roads or paths lead to heaven" comes from. If you quote this, you are talking about Hinduism.

The early Hindus never believed there was a heaven. In today's Hindu belief, heaven is one of several possible destinations for the soul after death, depending on how the individual has lived. The concept of heaven in Hinduism is called Svarga. It is believed to be a place of great joy and pleasure where the soul is reunited with loved ones and experiences the fruits of its good deeds. But if you fell short in life, you have to keep coming back to earth.

They believe in reincarnation, meaning you come back as something depending on your karma. Instead of heaven, you just keep coming back in the next life.

They firmly believe in patriarchy.

During my many cab rides in Singapore, it wasn't uncommon for the driver to have a statue on their dashboard representing whatever god they wanted some type of blessing from. They believe there are multiple gods (millions of divine beings), not just one. So, it is not unfathomable that they might accept Jesus as just another god and keep all the rest.

They are often seeking something but not seeing anything yet materialize from one of their gods. Sometimes, when their prayers are not being answered, they think they must be seeking the wrong god since there are over a million to choose from. In that case, they will consult with one of their holy people who then assigns them the right god to seek for what they want. If you can pray with them and meet their need, or if God chooses to intervene with the miraculous, it can open a door to discuss the One True God of heaven.

"They are often seeking something but not seeing anything yet materialize from one of their gods ... If you can pray with them and meet their need ... it can open a door to discuss the One True God of heaven."

PRIMER ON BUDDHISM

Buddhism, which comprises 6 percent of the world's population, is a philosophy based on the teachings of Buddha in Northern India, a teacher who lived between the fourth and sixth century BC, so over four hundred years before Jesus. It came at a time of great discontentment in the Hindu religion. Buddha's central teachings are that desire is the root cause of suffering and that people should seek to eliminate desire.

Buddha insisted he was human and that there was no Almighty God. Jesus many times claimed to be in the godhead as the Son of God, both human and divine, which we covered earlier in this chapter.

Out of this particular faith came terms we have culturally picked up over the years, such as "karma," which is like the biblical law of sowing and reaping; and "nirvana," which was the name of a rock band but it refers to the attainment of enlightenment through meditation and letting go of all attachments to be ultimately released from the cycle of reincarnation, which they call rebirth. Those who are reborn get to come back as one of six possible realms: gods, demi-gods, humans, animals, hungry ghosts, and hells.

> *This Book of the Law shall not depart from your mouth, but you shall meditate in it day and night, that you may observe to do according to all that is written in it. For then you will make your way prosperous, and then you will have good success.* (Joshua 1:8)

Meditation is also a biblical principle that dates back to the time of Moses—long before Buddha. Doing this in Christianity means you will be prosperous and succeed.

There are four truths in Buddhism:

1. The truth of suffering.
2. The truth of the cause of suffering.
3. The truth of the end of suffering.
4. The truth of the path that frees us from suffering.

Some Buddhist teachers describe themselves as people who have discovered the path. They firmly believe in patriarchy. There is no savior or road to salvation in Buddhism. Following this belief means denying the presence or reality of God.

"There is no savior or road to salvation in Buddhism. Following this belief means denying the presence or reality of God."

PRIMER ON SHINTOISM

Shintoism, which comprises 4 percent of the world's population, is primarily in Japan. They call it the way of *kami*, or divine beings, and they believe they are able to get divine power from interaction with these beings. The key beliefs in Shintoism are:

1. Veneration of *kami* (spirits or deities) believed to inhabit the natural world.
2. Reverence for nature.
3. Focus on purity and cleanliness.
4. Importance of ritual and ceremony.
5. No concept of original sin.
6. No transcendental other world.
7. Respect for family.
8. Sacredness of all life.
9. Ritual purification (misogi) for cleansing and renewal of the spirit.

Practitioners worship a divine power. Nature is an important part of worship, which is why they often practice devotions in beautiful settings with woods, trees, and gardens. They also use smoke from either incense or wood burning in their worship of divine beings. Shinto beliefs have been handed down through ages orally with no written tradition. They do believe in patriarchy.

HOW TO PRAY FOR OTHER RELIGIONS & ATHEISTS

Never get into a debate with people on their faith. Begin by binding that antichrist spirit off them. If you can get close enough to begin shining your light of Jesus upon them, then you can ask if there is something you could pray for them. Jesus said:

> *Let your light shine before men in such a way that they may see your good deeds and moral excellence, and [recognize and honor and] glorify your Father who is in heaven.* (Matthew 5:16 AMP)

Show them that you're happy and joyous and be willing to help them. This is the very definition of putting on Christ every day and shining so much that others are attracted to you.

People always have something in their life they are seeking, whether it is healing, finances, or other areas. Ask the Lord to give you the right words to say—ask for words of knowledge to speak things only they would know.

Pray for them to experience dreams and visions where Jesus reveals Himself so they become willing to turn to the Lord. Pray that they run into other people who have converted and who will talk with them about the Lord Jesus.

Marylin Hickey wrote a book titled *Dinner with Muhammad: A Surprising Look at a Beautiful Friendship*, where she talked about Muslims' attraction to signs, wonders, and miracles. She was even featured on CBS News in 2017 talking about this subject.

When you pray for these people, the Lord loves to show out and do exceedingly abundantly above all you can ask and think.

JEWISH PEOPLE

Jewish people comprise 3 percent of the world's population. For Jewish people who have not yet accepted Jesus as their Lord and Savior, it is God who has blinded their eyes.

> *But although He had done so many signs before them, they did not believe in Him, that the word of Isaiah the prophet might be fulfilled, which he spoke: "Lord, who has believed our report? And to whom has the arm of the Lord been revealed?" Therefore they could not believe, because Isaiah said again: "He has blinded their eyes and hardened their hearts, lest they should see with their eyes, lest they should understand with their hearts and turn, so that I should heal them." These things Isaiah said when he saw His glory and spoke of Him.* (John 12:37–41)

Talking about the veil that lies over their hearts "when Moses is read," II Corinthians 3:14–16 says:

> *But their minds were blinded. For until this day the same veil remains unlifted in the reading of the Old Testament, because the veil is taken away in Christ. But even to this day, when Moses is read, a veil lies on their heart. Nevertheless when one turns to the Lord, the veil is taken away.*

They have lost the ability to understand until or unless the veil is removed; however, some Jews actually accepted Jesus as the Christ during events recorded in the Book of Acts and beyond. There are a lot of traditions that have been handed down from generation to generation teaching that their

Savior (Messiah) is yet to come, but understanding is possible if you ask the Lord to remove the veil.

We always have to remember that the Old Testament was written by Jewish people. The New Testament church started with Jewish people. It wasn't until Acts 10 that a non-Jewish person by the name of Cornelius received an answer to prayer that he and his whole household was saved.

Every day, more and more Jewish people accept Jesus as their Lord and Savior.

Jewish ministers who have accepted Jesus are sometimes referred to as Messianic Jews. Sid Roth is one of those ministers who travels to Israel and other Jewish parts of the world. He mentioned recently that signs, wonders, and miracles break out in his services, and Jewish people are having dreams of Jesus.

A Sample Prayer for Jewish People to Be Saved

Father, in the name of Jesus, I ask that You take the blinders off of the eyes of the Jewish people who have not yet accepted You. However You need to—do it. Cause dreams, witnesses, and other means. Cause them to come to the knowledge of the truth that Jesus is their Lord and Savior. We rebuke the tradition and stubbornness that will keep them from seeking You out. You told them early on that if they seek You, You will be found. In Jesus's name, hearts be open to the truth of Jesus.

RELIGIONS THAT ELEVATE THE APOSTLES' CREED AND CHURCH ATTENDANCE

Some religious expressions of Christianity teach or give the impression that salvation is in either reciting the right words or showing up to regular church services. There are many Catholic and Protestant churches that recite the Apostles' Creed or something like it in their services, and there is nothing wrong with that.

The question is whether those people have accepted Jesus as their Lord and Savior. When I was a Catholic, if someone had asked me whether I confessed Jesus as my Lord and Savior, I would have said, "Yes. We do that every service."

I learned to change the question to: "Do you have an intimate relationship with the Lord Jesus?" I now distinguish between a confession versus a personal relationship. If they stutter on that, then I ask if I could pray with them to have Jesus come into their heart and ignite a personal relationship with Him.

If they allow you to do that, then you will see their face suddenly change as the love of God manifests in their hearts.

APOSTLES' CREED (CATHOLIC VERSION)

The Catholics recite:

I believe in God the Father, almighty Creator of heaven and earth, and in Jesus Christ, his only Son, our Lord, who was conceived by the Holy Spirit, born of the Virgin Mary, suffered under Pontius Pilate, was crucified, died and was buried; he descended into hell; on the third day he rose again from the dead; he ascended into heaven, and is seated at the right hand of God the Father almighty; from there he will come to judge the living and the dead. I believe in the Holy Spirit, the holy catholic Church, the communion of saints, the forgiveness of sins, the resurrection of the body, and life everlasting. Amen.

WISDOM FROM VICKI

The Lord will bring people into my thinking as an indication that I need to pray for them. I can either pray in English or in the Spirit, depending upon what the Lord says to do.

There are times when I will ask the Lord, "Is there anything or anyone You want me to pray about to further Your kingdom?"

One day, I felt an urgency to pray but didn't sense anything specific. Later, I asked what that was about. He said, "I needed you to help bring souls into My kingdom through your willingness to pray."

The Lord is no respecter of persons. He will use whoever is willing.

Chapter 3

Persistent Prayer Is Key

During trips to the United Kingdom, I often took a couple of days just to walk around, recover from jet lag, and see the sights of London and Edinburgh. I knew to bring jackets of varying weights because the North Sea wind could send chills right through me even with temperatures at over seventy degrees. I love the pictures I see online of sunny days in England or Scotland because those days are rare. Umbrellas are a must.

The British and Scots are known for preserving history. Although the buildings have been converted for other uses, many in that part of the world are more than four hundred years old. Walking and observing, I could feel the lethargic spiritual climate, as if this place was once filled with life but the people had since grown cold to the things of God.

On one particular trip, I couldn't help but notice that many of the signs posted by old buildings had once belonged to churches. These houses of worship and prayer were converted to pubs, libraries, bookstores, and New Age auditoriums, but the signs that donned them documented massive revivals and moves of God, times when the fire of God fell and thousands of people were brought into the kingdom.

I read in a book on church history that, during that period, church attendance in Britain had dwindled. The English church as it existed was going through the motions, so many of the people—the living body of Christ—started meeting in basements just to pray for the services and ultimately for the community. As they persisted, they noticed the power of God changing the hearts of the people and then impacting the greater community. In one instance, events that started in Wales moved through Scotland and England. A new trend broke out with some church meetings being preceded by hours of gathered prayer. Communities were so dramatically impacted that the townspeople erected signs in front of these powerful churches to mark and memorialize them. And there I stood bearing witness through those old signs reminding me of God's faithfulness to answer our prayers. I asked the Lord if I could visit this country again. He responded, "Where My fire once fell, it can fall again." No person or society is ever beyond the reach of our Savior and Lord, Jesus.

"Their heartfelt prayers caused them to care deeply and become hungry for action on behalf of all the lost people at all levels of society."

What did these saints pray for? They started by praying for the church staff, so desperately needed, and continued with prayers for the local community and the nation at large. Their prayers were God's preparation for their own hearts to be made ready for the incoming harvest as their heartfelt prayers caused them to care deeply and become hungry for action on behalf of all the lost people at all levels of society.

> *Now this is the confidence that we have in Him, that if we ask anything according to His will, He hears us. And if we know that He hears us, whatever we ask, we know that we have the petitions that we have asked of Him.* (1 John 5:14-15)

When you start praying for lost people, God 100 percent approves that prayer. God then intervenes by the Holy Spirit to help guide your prayers more effectively. Soon, laborers swing into action and the harvest begins just as in the Book of Acts where thousands were added to the church after the people gathered and prayed. Jesus said:

> *Ask and **keep on** asking and it will be given to you; seek and **keep on** seeking and you will find; knock and keep on knocking and the door will be opened to you. For everyone who **keeps on** asking receives, and he who **keeps on** seeking finds, and to him who **keeps on** knocking, it will be opened.* (Matthew 7:7–8 AMP, emphasis mine)

Powerful prayers are not vain and repetitious but from the heart. Sometimes I pray once and I'm astonished that nothing happened. Is God hard of hearing or playing hard to get? No, sometimes there are demonic forces working hard to distract us. Sometimes God just wants us to come spend time with Him and not just bark at Him a drive-by prayer.

In Luke 11, Jesus talked about the Lord's prayer. He followed that brief discourse with:

> *Which of you shall have a friend, and go to him at midnight and say to him, "Friend, lend me three loaves; for a friend of mine has come to me on his journey, and I have nothing to set before him"; and he will answer from within and say, "Do not trouble me; the door is now shut, and my children are with me in bed; I cannot rise and give to you"? I say to you, though he will not rise and give to him because he is his friend, yet because of his* **persistence** *he will rise and give him as many as he needs.* (Luke 11:5–8, emphasis mine)

Jesus was teaching us persistence. You ask and you keep on asking.

Another word used for "persistence" is "boldness." The AMPC version of verse 8 says:

> *I tell you, although he will not get up and supply him anything because he is his friend, yet because of his shameless persistence and insistence he will get up and give him as much as he needs.*

Come to your Father who loves and does good for you. Ask boldly for what you need—but in this book, what we "need" is souls for His kingdom.

So, if I ask and keep on asking, how do I know when to stop? You keep after it until you see breakthrough. In fact, anyone in the ministry will tell you that persistent prayer is key to any move of God. He wants us to press in and catch His compassion for people. He wants us to see the people around us, lost and hurting, and know that we have the answer. He wants us to swing into action knowing He will give us the words to say.

> *Ask of Me, and I will give You the nations for Your inheritance, and the ends of the earth for Your possession.* (Psalm 2:8)

The first key word in this verse is "nations," which is typically rendered people or people groups. The second key word is "ask," which means God wants us to inquire, seek counsel for, or demand. When you are asking something that is God's will, it gives Him the opportunity to help guide you in how to pray.

So, persistence is required. Praying for others' salvation is not just a one-time thing. It is not us waiting on God but God waiting on us.

> *Yet you don't have what you want because you don't ask God for it. And even when you ask, you don't get it because your motives are all wrong—you want only what will give you pleasure.* (James 4:2–3 NLT)

When we choose to be persistent, praying for the lost comes to the forefront of our mind every day.

To pray God's will over someone, I start with Scriptures that clearly show me what He wants. As we discussed in chapter two, He desires everyone to be saved and to come to the knowledge of the truth. Praying for salvation is not a prayer in vain based on someone's whim, but 100 percent in the will of God.

Prayer is an open conversation with the Lord. I'm not a particularly talkative person, but when I am praying to the Lord, I tend to dominate the discussion. One of my pastors painted a picture for me: imagine someone who knows nothing doing all the talking with someone who knows all things and can do all things.

I am still learning to stop and listen for what He has to say. How about you?

You may outline steps, but the Lord can shortcut your path to success. All you need do is ask and, in all your asking, ask for direction. Let Him guide and instruct your thoughts and prayers. He wants conversation and wants to grow an intimate relationship with you.

Where there is resistance in receiving answered prayer, it is not God you are battling with. The person you are praying for has free will. They can decide to go back to their old life. God desires all people to be saved. But we have an adversary who is busy working against us. The adversary might show up as an invitation from an old friend inviting them back to the old party. That "friend" may know the right words to persuade the person to abandon their new life with Christ and reengage with sin and slavery. We might think it is just coincidental that their old friends keep resurfacing, but that is no coincidence. It is the same old devil using the same old tricks. The new convert may not notice the impact on them when smelling those same aromas, hearing the sounds, and seeing the sights as they approach that old bar. Everyone inside appears to be having a great time. That appearance is false and the people may even be actively lying, trying hard to pull others back into sin and despair, but the Good News says:

We are not fighting against flesh-and-blood enemies, but against evil rulers and authorities of the unseen world, against mighty powers in this dark world, and against evil spirits in the heavenly places. (Ephesians 6:12 NLT)

There is a fight for that person's soul, and on the other side of that fight are powers and spirits "of the unseen world." The demonic realm will always try to hide behind people, using them to recapture the saved soul to captivity. It may not be obvious, but the words and actions coming from that person should alert us. It is not flesh and blood but evil that is trying to rule over this person. We must take authority over that spirit and bring them into the kingdom of God, where it is their birthright to dwell and be blessed.

People should pray always and never give up.

Remind yourself constantly: this is a fight you will win—if you don't give up. In Luke 18:1–8, Jesus spells out the story of the persistent widow. I love Luke's dissertation, telling you the object of the lesson before the story is told. He says:

*One day Jesus told his disciples a story to show that they should always pray and never give up. "There was a judge in a certain city," he said, "who neither feared God nor cared about people. A widow of that city came to him repeatedly, saying, 'Give me justice in this dispute with my enemy.' The judge ignored her for a while, but finally he said to himself, 'I don't fear God or care about people, but this woman is driving me crazy. I'm going to see that she gets justice, because she is wearing me out with her constant requests!'" Then the Lord said, "Learn a lesson from this unjust judge. Even he rendered a just decision in the end. So don't you think God will surely give justice to his chosen people who **cry out to him day*** *and night? Will he keep putting them off? I tell you, he will grant justice to them quickly! But when the Son of Man returns, how many will he find on the earth who have faith?"* (Luke 18:1–8 NLT, emphasis mine)

This woman wanted something done and she needed the judge to do it, but the judge could not care less that this lady had a problem. He decided to ignore her in hopes that she would go away. Nevertheless, the woman made up her mind to return daily until she got what she came for. Finally, realizing this lady was never going to stop "wearing" him out, he granted her request.

The judge in this story represents the demonic realm that is trying to maintain a hold on the person or people you are praying for, and they are not going to give in unless you force their hand. Like the persistent widow, you keep pounding the demonic realm until they let go. There is no place in this for a "give up" attitude. Your attitude must be: I am going to fight until I win.

Remember, we are instructed to be persistent, which means: "persisting, especially in spite of opposition, obstacles, discouragement, etc. Lasting or enduring tenaciously."[2]

"Persistent" is synonymous with "perseverance" but implies steadfastness and endurance, being fixed, immovable, and steady in direction.[3]

For the word of God is living and powerful, and sharper than any two-edged sword, piercing even to the division

2   Dictionary.com, s.v. "Persistent," accessed April 7, 2025, https://www.dictionary.com/browse/persistent
3   Dictionary.com, s.v. "Steadfastness," accessed April 7, 2025, https://www.dictionary.com/browse/steadfastness

of soul and spirit, and of joints and marrow, and is a discerner of the thoughts and intents of the heart. (Hebrews 4:12)

We must develop the habit of praying what the Word says about people. Every day, you are going after this person's spirit to see that they turn toward the truth of the Good News. You continue to pray for them until you see the person or people turn to the Lord.

Ephesians also talks about a "sword of the Spirit," which is the Word of God and praying with perseverance (persistence).

And take the helmet of salvation, and the sword of the Spirit, which is the word of God; praying always with all prayer and supplication in the Spirit, being watchful to this end with all perseverance and supplication for all the saints. (Ephesians 6:17–18)

A double-edged sword has two sharpened edges that cut going in and going out. It cuts going up and going down. The Word of God and the sword of the Spirit are an unbeatable force against the demonic realm. The adversary may act like it has no effect, but persistently praying the Word over someone will in time wear down the most stubborn demonic spirit. The Word released from our mouth in prayer for someone cuts away the hold of the demonic realm.

We have to remember that the greater power is in us. We will win if we do not give up.

But you belong to God, my dear children. You have already won a victory over those people, because the Spirit who lives in you is greater than the spirit who lives in the world. (I John 4:4 NLT)

The Amplified Bible says, "He who is in you is greater than he (Satan)," which is the demonic realm. The word "greater" is talking about rank and power. We have the victory, and when we take on an "I will not give up" spirit just like the persistent widow, we will see the victory. I usually pray according to this Scripture:

> *What is the conclusion then? I will pray with the spirit, and I will also pray with the understanding. I will sing with the spirit, and I will also sing with the understanding.* (I Corinthians 14:15)

Seeking God's wisdom and direction throughout this process is a major key to victory. The Holy Spirit is in you to guide you into all truth and, many times, to help redirect your prayers so they are more effective. Over time, this helps you to develop a greater ability to hear His voice and understand His heart of love for people.

WISDOM FROM VICKI

Don't give up praying when you don't see the results. God wants them saved and delivered more than you do. I saw my father and mother give their lives to the Lord in their older years. God said through the prophet Jeremiah:

> *"The prophet who has a dream, let him tell a dream; and he who has My word, let him speak My word faithfully. What is the chaff to the wheat?" says the LORD. "Is not My word like a fire?" says the LORD, "And like a hammer that breaks the rock in pieces?"* (Jeremiah 23:28–29)

Persistent Prayer Is Key

The AMPC version of verse 29 says it this way:

> *Is not My word like fire [that consumes all that cannot endure the test]? says the LORD, and like a hammer that breaks in pieces the rock [of most stubborn resistance]?*

The pictured painted in verse 29 is a rock being hit repeatedly with a hammer, which symbolizes the Word of God spoken out of your mouth. It looks like it's not moving or breaking but you keep hitting it again and again. Then, suddenly, the most stubborn rock breaks into pieces. When His Word is spoken, it consumes the wicked things and purifies the good. The hammer of the Word breaks the rock so that it ultimately shatters pride and stubbornness into pieces. Then, as if all of a sudden, manifestation occurs.

> *For the weapons of our warfare are not physical [weapons of flesh and blood], but they are mighty before God for the overthrow and destruction of strongholds.* (II Corinthians 10:4 AMPC)

His Word coming out of your mouth on a continual basis destroys strongholds in a person's life. It is like a rock that breaks up the most stubborn rock of resistance, so just keep going and never give up! Never give up. Just keep banging away until your answer comes. This is what it means to be persistent.

Chapter 4

Step One:
Bind the Enemy
Off of Their Minds

When you travel in airports a lot, you grow somewhat numb to delays, especially for those short-haul flights in the United States like Dallas to Houston. If it's a weather or mechanical delay, I thank the flight crew for not trying to push past it crossing their fingers that it all works out. When people berate the agent as if that person was in charge of the airline, the atmosphere can get charged with negativity quickly. Believers can be equally guilty of this. We have to be aware of Satan's devices. He'll often use minor irritations like delayed flights or long lines to push the envelope and take believers out by provoking them to rash decisions and words.

What do you do when the whole country of France decides to shut the airports down in sympathy to other unions, and you're in Scotland trying to get to France? Why do we get so angry? It just makes things worse when you scream at people. Why are churchgoers saying hateful things? How can people raised up in the faith come off so ugly and disrespectful? Why do most of the other faiths hate Christians? What is going on with people? You could start a whole talk show just based on that title, but we have all been guilty of saying things we wish would evaporate out of the air like it never happened. If you are ever going to take authority and control over the spiritual atmosphere, you have to bind the enemy off your mind first.

We now have social media and podcasts that are not evil in and of themselves, but where people feel emboldened to say and do things behind a camera or a phone that they wouldn't normally say or do. What is driving this behavior? Some people are craving attention. Some of it is tied to loneliness, which we are seeing in our time at epidemic proportions. For others, they're just cooking up click bait, while still others have not seriously considered the implications of their choice of lifestyle and demeanor.

"If you are ever going to take authority and control over the spiritual atmosphere, you have to bind the enemy off your mind first."

When I was growing up attending Catholic school, one of the nuns (from hell) woke me up with a vivid picture of two beings on my shoulder. One good angel tells me the right thing to do; the second, a little devil, tells me what I really wanted to do. It is a simple example that does have some truth to it.

Step One: Bind the Enemy Off of Their Minds

We do have free will but we also are in the midst of unseen influences trying to direct our decisions. The most horrible mass murderers often confess that they heard voices encouraging them to do what they did. That is an extreme example, but all people are in the midst of suggestions coming to their mind all the time. When you see people lying continuously or demonstrating violence to the point of murder, remember that Jesus identified the spirit that is influencing them:

You are of your father the devil, and the desires of your father you want to do. He was a murderer from the beginning, and does not stand in the truth, because there is no truth in him. When he speaks a lie, he speaks from his own resources, for he is a liar and the father of it. (John 8:44)

Scripture also refers to the devil as "the accuser of our brethren":

Then I heard a loud voice saying in heaven, "Now salvation, and strength, and the kingdom of our God, and the power of His Christ have come, for the accuser of our brethren, who accused them before our God day and night, has been cast down." (Revelation 12:10)

The demonic realm's job is to minimize or eliminate your impact while you are here on the earth. Sometimes I'm amazed at myself falling for the same routine and bothering to get angry, just thinking, Déjà vu all over again. I have come to recognize more quickly when I am being attacked by a spirit of accusation. If someone is falsely accusing me repeatedly, an accusing spirit is trying to be in control. The devil is a liar and he likes to halt people that are taking action by using false or exaggerated accusations.

Jesus said there are two kingdoms—the kingdom of God and the kingdom of this world. The kingdom of God came to set people free from those caught in the kingdom of this world. The kingdom of this world is ruled by the Satan and the demonic realm. For those who wonder why we don't talk about the "Kingdom of Me"—there are only two kingdoms for us to consider. We are either being influenced by and yielded to one or the other.

Here are some of the attributes of both kingdoms:

Christ *Kingdom of God*	Antichrist *Kingdom of the World*
Jesus is King	Satan is king
The name of Jesus is superior authority	Liar and father of lies
Sets people free	Binds the minds
Life more abundantly	Steals, kills, and destroys
Authority over the demonic realm	Violence and confusion
Love	Accuser of the brethren
Intimate relationship with God	Lawlessness
Joy	Depression, worry, and dread
Forgiveness	Hatred
Holy Spirit guides us	Demonic realm guides us

Jesus gave us authority over the demonic realm, which is from the kingdom of this world. The name of Jesus effectively used by the believer carries power to run off demonic spirits, and not only those bothering us but also the people we are praying for.

Step One: Bind the Enemy Off of Their Minds

Then the seventy returned with joy, saying, "Lord, even the demons are subject to us in Your name." And He said to them, "I saw Satan fall like lightning from heaven. Behold, I give you the authority to trample on serpents and scorpions, and over all the power of the enemy, and nothing shall by any means hurt you. Nevertheless do not rejoice in this, that the spirits are subject to you, but rather rejoice because your names are written in heaven." (Luke 10:17–20)

Serpents and scorpions represent the demonic realm and Jesus gave us authority over them. A simple definition of "authority" is the power or right to give orders, make decisions, and enforce obedience. This means you have the right to force demonic spirits to go in Jesus's name. He gave us His name to pray with. His name is more powerful than any force in the universe.

Let this mind be in you which was also in Christ Jesus, who, being in the form of God, did not consider it robbery to be equal with God, but made Himself of no reputation, taking the form of a bondservant, and coming in the likeness of men. And being found in appearance as a man, He humbled Himself and became obedient to the point of death, even the death of the cross. Therefore God also has highly exalted Him and given Him the name which is above every name, that at the name of Jesus every knee should bow, of those in heaven, and of those on earth, and of those under the earth, and that every tongue should confess that Jesus Christ is Lord, to the glory of God the Father. (Philippians 2:5–11)

When the Scripture above says His name is "above every name," it means that His rank is superior to anything in heaven, on the earth, or under the earth. Every knee has to bow and every tongue must confess that Jesus is Lord to the glory of God the Father.

Jesus has authorized us to use His name, which is more than enough to cause the demonic realm to flee—but the words have to come out of our mouth to enforce the name.

Their minds are blinded.

The Bible refers to unseen spiritual forces trying to sway us one way or another. When we give our heart to the Lord, the Holy Spirit enters our spirit to help guide us in being more like Jesus. The Holy Spirit is our guide but does not control our every move.

> *If the Good News we preach is hidden behind a veil, it is hidden only from people who are perishing. Satan, who is the god of this world, has blinded the minds of those who don't believe. They are unable to see the glorious light of the Good News. They don't understand this message about the glory of Christ, who is the exact likeness of God.* (II Corinthians 4:3–4 NLT)

According to this Scripture, Satan, who is the god of this world, can blind us from the truth. A veil covers the eyes to the point of blindness. Like leading a person with blinders on—they won't see the truth until the blinders are taken away. The veil is held there by Satan, whose name means "adversary" because he is against us. We have to remove Satan's blinders so they can see and know the truth. God sends you to preach the Good News:

Step One: Bind the Enemy Off of Their Minds

To open their eyes, so they may turn from darkness to light and from the power of Satan to God. Then they will receive forgiveness for their sins and be given a place among God's people, who are set apart by faith in me. (Acts 26:18 NLT)

This is your hope and goal in sharing the Good News—open their eyes so they can see the truth. Whether you preach at Walmart or bring them to church, the preaching of the Good News is essential to their salvation, but it typically takes prayer to first remove the blinders.

I know it is popular to believe Satan and the demonic realm don't really exist, as if hell is a wooden club used by the church to keep people in line, but you have to stop and ask—if man is made in the image and likeness of God who is Life and who is infinitely and inherently good, and man is equally capable of shooting, murdering, massacring, stealing, and destroying, is it possible there are unseen demonic forces and influences at play, manipulating, and, at times, even possessing us?

CHOOSING A LIFE OF SIN

Run from anything that stimulates youthful lusts. Instead, pursue righteous living, faithfulness, love, and peace. Enjoy the companionship of those who call on the Lord with pure hearts. Again I say, don't get involved in foolish, ignorant arguments that only start fights. A servant of the Lord must not quarrel but must be kind to everyone, be able to teach, and be patient with difficult people. Gently instruct those who oppose the truth. Perhaps God will change those people's hearts, and they will learn the truth. Then they will come to their senses and escape from the devil's trap. For they have been held captive by him to do whatever he wants. (II Timothy 2:22–26 NLT)

Every born-again person faces the temptation to go back to their old ways. Should one choose to enjoy the practices of their youth as before they were saved, they have fallen into the devil's trap. The devil holds them captive to do with them whatever he wants. We see this with drugs, alcohol, sex outside of marriage, pornography, and other unhealthy choices. This is why people who appear to live an upstanding life "suddenly" fall mightily and their sins are exposed. How did they get there? Daily choices.

Typically, the Lord will send people to help them get back on the path, but in the end, it will be their choice. People will listen to those they know and trust.

Those who have been born into God's family do not make a practice of sinning, because God's life is in them. So they can't keep on sinning, because they are children of God. So now we can tell who are children of God and who are children of the devil. Anyone who does not live righteously and does not love other believers does not belong to God. (I John 3:9–10 NLT)

If you get saved but continue making a practice of sinning as if nothing happened during your salvation experience, then you have to question whether you ever got saved. Sometimes people just say a prayer and think they are good to go, but there needs to be a heart change. The heart change doesn't mean you are suddenly perfect, but it does mean that you are no longer "at home" with sin and you respond with a repentant heart in the face of it. For example, after getting saved I didn't feel anything in particular "happen" to me, but I noticed all my cussing disappeared. I was good at cussing, but it just vanished—and it took me a lot less time to say anything. I was baffled for a few days, but I had to conclude something had changed and it was due to my salvation experience.

"Whether you preach at Walmart or bring them to church, the preaching of the Good News is essential to their salvation, but it typically takes prayer to first remove the blinders."

Again, this does not mean we never experience temptation and occasionally stumble, but stumbling causes the born-again believer "godly sorrow," which is spiritual pain in our heart because the Holy Spirit who lives in our heart is letting us know when something is not okay. If, instead of resisting the sin, the person resists the Holy Spirit, the impact of that Holy Spirit "heart check" becomes less and less. Eventually, that sin may run its full course. That is why it is critical for people to remain in the body of believers, which we refer to as a church, to check on each other, strengthen one another, and hold each other accountable.

For such are false apostles, deceitful workers, transforming themselves into apostles of Christ. And no wonder! For Satan himself transforms himself into an angel of light. Therefore it is no great thing if his ministers also transform themselves into ministers of righteousness, whose end will be according to their works. (II Corinthians 11:13–15)

Satan often appears as an angel of light. He transforms—or disguises—himself as an angel of light. That means he may tell you something that sounds good, but it doesn't line up with what Jesus said.

When people start preaching that there are many roads to heaven, for example, it may sound nice to the those listening but it is no more or less than a denial that Jesus is the Christ.

That's why it is so important for all of us to spend time with Him and His Word. Then, we will be able to discern wrong teachings. False doctrines typically come across subtly. If you start hearing things that don't align with the Good News gospel, then go to another church.

When you read the primers on Islam, Buddhism, Hinduism, and Shintoism provided in this book, how could you argue with some of the principles? They are close to what the Bible says, but none of them acknowledge that Jesus is the Christ.

Who is a liar but he who denies that Jesus is the Christ? He is antichrist who denies the Father and the Son. Whoever denies the Son does not have the Father either; he who acknowledges the Son has the Father also. (I John 2:22–23)

Beloved, do not believe every spirit, but test the spirits, whether they are of God; because many false prophets have gone out into the world. By this you know the Spirit of God: Every spirit that confesses that Jesus Christ has come in the flesh is of God, and every spirit that does not confess that Jesus Christ has come in the flesh is not of God. And this is the spirit of the Antichrist, which you have heard was coming, and is now already in the world. (I John 4:1–3)

We are supposed to test the spirits. The test is two-pronged:

1. Every spirit that confesses Jesus came in the flesh is of God.
2. Every spirit who denies that Jesus is the Christ denies the Son and the Father. This is the spirit of antichrist.

None of the other religions acknowledge that Jesus is the Christ or that He came in the flesh.

Who is speaking through a person teaching false doctrines? Are their words lining up with Scripture?

Now the Spirit expressly says that in latter times some will depart from the faith, giving heed to deceiving spirits and doctrines of demons, speaking lies in hypocrisy, having their own conscience seared with a hot iron, forbidding to marry, and commanding to abstain from foods which God created to be received with thanksgiving by those who believe and know the truth. For every creature of God is good, and nothing is to be refused if it is received with thanksgiving; for it is sanctified by the word of God and prayer. (I Timothy 4:1–5)

When you look at Islam, Buddhism, Hinduism, and Shintoism and ask yourself what is wrong with those beliefs, the answer is nothing—except that they deny that Jesus is the Christ. And eventually the nice sounding words and platitudes will turn to murder and rage aimed at Christians and Jews.

How do we deal with antichrist spirits? Jesus gave us authority over them with His name and His Word. The Bible refers to binding and loosing in two different ways—one with the demonic realm and the other with a believer who is in sin.

> *But if I cast out demons by the Spirit of God, surely the kingdom of God has come upon you. Or how can one enter a strong man's house and plunder his goods, unless he first **binds the strong man**? And then he will plunder his house.* (Matthew 12:28–29, emphasis mine)

The next Scripture is dealing with a believer who is in sin, giving them a chance to repent.

> *Assuredly, I say to you, whatever you bind on earth will be bound in heaven, and whatever you loose on earth will be loosed in heaven.* (Matthew 18:18)

In both cases He uses the word "bind," but in Matthew 12 He is talking about the ability to tie someone up so you can ransack the devil's prized possessions—namely, the person you are praying for.

In Matthew 18, He is saying that whatever you declare improper and unlawful is improper and unlawful in heaven. That means heaven and earth need to be in agreement with what is proper for there to be order and power.

Matthew 12 teaches that we can bind the devil who is causing someone to be blinded by using the name of Jesus.

WISDOM FROM VICKI

I have to make deposits of His Word in my heart so I can be effective in what I'm doing. That means I have to stop, read, and listen to Scripture until it overflows. Don't talk about what you see; talk about what you believe.

"Don't talk about what you see; talk about what you believe."

When you pray, expect something to happen. Expectation is commonly referred to as biblical hope. It works along with faith and love to produce great power.

Don't be moved by the great temptation to quit, waiver, or doubt. When I am praying for people, I let the Word of God fight its own fight by speaking the Scriptures. His Word never fails:

> *For as the rain comes down, and the snow from heaven, and do not return there, but water the earth, and make it bring forth and bud, that it may give seed to the sower and bread to the eater, so shall My word be that goes forth from My mouth; it shall not return to Me void, but it shall accomplish what I please, and it shall prosper in the thing for which I sent it. (Isaiah 55:10–11)*

His Word coming out of your mouth in prayer will not return without producing the intended effect. It means you're having an impact and just like the hammer that breaks the rock of most stubborn resistance, we keep binding the devil off of the person you are praying for until they come into the saving knowledge of Jesus.

We must take authority over the adversary to bring that person or people group into the kingdom of God. The demonic realm does not give up easily. Be persistent with your prayers. You have to force the "strong man" to take his hands off of them. When you fight and don't give up, you will win.

A Sample Prayer

Father, in the name of Jesus, You have given us authority to tread on scorpions and serpents and over all the power of the enemy. I come against the devil that is blinding the eyes of and I command him off of so he or she has the opportunity to hear the Good News. Devil, you can't stop this person from being saved in Jesus's name.

Chapter 5

Step Two:
Loose the Holy Spirit

One destination I always enjoyed was Singapore. I have never known a cold day in Singapore. Their nearness to the equator means temperatures do not vary much. Umbrellas are always necessary as there is a rainy season and, like Houston, it usually rains at least once a day.

It was a great business environment and one of the few countries where I felt completely safe to go walking around. Unfortunately, the government not only sanctions but promotes prostitution. After hours, the island comes alive with entertainment of the wholesome as well as the unwholesome kind. So, after dinner, I would retreat into my hotel room to avoid getting hit up by prostitutes. On the bright side, it gave me time to do a lot of praying and reading.

The island is comprised of three main religions: Buddhism, Christianity, and Islam. Singapore as a country and culture is happy to have a balance of religions. They really don't want any one of them to get the upper hand. The spiritual climate had some life, but a mixture of different spirits including a deeply embedded controlling spirit—you're being recorded all the time.

Drivers are on the left-hand side of the road and the traffic there is horrible, so I take cab rides to get around. Many times, the cab drivers are of the Hindu faith. You can tell because they usually display a statue of their god or goddess on the dashboard. As I mentioned earlier, their chosen deity represents what the person is hoping the false god will bring to pass in their life. Popular idols include the goddess of love and the goddess of fertility, but there are too many gods to keep up with. The challenge with Hindus is that they are happy to just add to their dashboard another God named Jesus.

Singapore as well as all countries need a mighty move of God in their government as well as the people. It can be a challenge to pray with the Hindu people and understand how to talk with them about the One True God, Jesus, but God knows how. He says He will give you the words to say.

SPIRITUAL FORCES AT PLAY

At times while praying for people, I have led them to rebuke the demonic from their own mouth. What do you suppose has typically come back to me in response? Often, the person immediately becomes more foul and vile than when we first started. Sometimes, the person actually gets better for a few days but then turns back to their old ways with foul intensity.

It's easy to get shaken up when things initially worsen, but the believer knows that when this happens, you are right over the target. You have stirred the devil's resting place and he doesn't like it. Naturally, he's going to react with foulness. He wants you to stop!

"It's easy to get shaken up with things initially worsen, but the believer knows that when this happens, you are right over the target."

Therefore, once you complete the first step, I strongly advise you to move on to the second step quickly. Why? Because that spirit has only temporarily cleared out. Jesus taught us about this when he explained:

> When an unclean spirit goes out of a man, he goes through dry places, seeking rest; and finding none, he says, "I will return to my house from which I came." And when he comes, he finds it swept and put in order. Then he goes and takes with him seven other spirits more wicked than himself, and they enter and dwell there; and the last state of that man is worse than the first. (Luke 11:24–26)

Once the unclean spirit has left and the house is "swept and put in order," you want to catch that moment of opportunity to help invite God into their life and into the space the demonic once occupied— before it comes back with seven more!

THE HELPER—THE HOLY SPIRIT

God through the Holy Spirit will not just fill someone without an invitation or another with authority helping to clear the way. He's not a God who acts like that. The devil is the one that forces his way in when a door is open. Jesus Himself said this plainly in John 10:10:

> *The thief does not come except to steal, and to kill, and to destroy. I have come that they may have life, and that they may have it more abundantly.*

The same verse in the NLT versions says:

> *The thief's purpose is to steal and kill and destroy. My purpose is to give them a rich and satisfying life.*

The choice of life or death ultimately belongs to the individual, but we also have the ability to sway someone's choice through prayer and action.

When binding things in the spirit, we want to simultaneously loose other spiritual forces to move into the person's life. To "loose" means to permit, declare lawful, or declare that something is allowed. In the next two Scriptures, we see Jesus giving His disciples (that would be us) "the keys of the kingdom." A believer has the authority to bind and loose through their words.

> *And I will give you the keys of the kingdom of heaven, and whatever you bind on earth will be bound in heaven, and whatever you loose on earth will be loosed in heaven.* (Matthew 16:19)

> *All authority has been given to Me in heaven and on earth. Go therefore and make disciples of all the nations, baptizing them in the name of the Father and of the Son and of the Holy Spirit.* (Matthew 28:18–19)

Step Two: Loose the Holy Spirit

Also read:

- Matthew 18:18–20
- Mark 16:14–20
- Luke 24:46–49
- John 20:21–23
- Acts 1:4–8

When you put all these Scriptures together, you get a clearer picture of what we have been commissioned to do. These verses give us our job description until He returns. I've been in corporate meetings where someone orders (short version), "Go get this done." I then ask questions about any limitations of scope, budgets, desired outcome, or things I need to be aware of before I go to task. If they say something like, "Just make this happen," then I know they have given me authority to carry out their desire. Authority carries power, and we have to be willing to pick up His authority to use it.

Going back to first base—the Helper, the Holy Spirit, has certain responsibilities. He will not intrude or enter into someone's life without an invitation from someone with the authority to open that door. So, after we take authority and bind up the spirits that are harassing and blinding people from the truth, we need to loose something that will start them on the road to Jesus. That "something" is actually a someone—the Holy Spirit.

> *But now I go away to Him who sent Me, and none of you asks Me, "Where are You going?" But because I have said these things to you, sorrow has filled your heart. Nevertheless I tell you the truth. It is to your advantage that I go away; for if I do not go away, **the Helper** will*

*not come to you; but if I depart, I will send Him to you. And when He has come, He will **convict the world** of sin, and of righteousness, and of judgment: of sin, because **they do not believe in Me**; of righteousness, because I go to My Father and you see Me no more; of judgment, because the ruler of this world is judged.* (John 16:5–11, emphasis mine)

Let's define who the Helper is.

But the Helper, the Holy Spirit, whom the Father will send in My name, He will teach you all things, and bring to your remembrance all things that I said to you. (John 14:26)

In John chapters 14 through 17, Jesus describes the Helper that will come take Jesus's place after He ascends into heaven. The Savior refers to the work of the Helper using the word "convict." This conviction is like an act of convincing you that you are in error—or on the wrong road. The non-believer often experiences this convincing as a desire for more truth. They start questioning life and attempting to change. Where it says that He will bring conviction to "the world," that phrase now refers to those who have not accepted Jesus as their Lord and Savior.

CONVICTS THE WORLD OF SIN

One of the many roles of the Holy Spirit is to convict the world of sin. John 16:8 says that the world will be convicted of sin "because they do not believe in Me." If someone is committing all kinds of sins such as stealing, adultery, murder, or whatever, there is still only one thing that will send them into eternal damnation. According to this verse, it is not

the stealing, adultery, murder, or whatever. Only the sin of unbelief in Jesus as Lord and Savior will send people into eternal damnation.

CONVICTS SINNERS TO MOVE TOWARD RIGHTEOUSNESS

The second role of the Holy Spirit is also mentioned in John 16:8. He will convict, or convince, sinners to move toward righteousness. Righteousness is agreement and right standing with God. Most people recognize in their heart that right and wrong exist, but He wants all people to know there is a right way to God, and the Holy Spirit is our Helper to find that way and live a life of righteousness.

CONVICTS THE WORLD OF JUDGMENT

The third role of the Holy Spirit is to convict the world of judgment. During every person's life, the Lord will warn them that judgment is coming if they do not change. Jesus is that Judge because all judgment has been given over to the Son. The god of this world has already been judged—his ultimate destiny is in the lake of fire. Anyone who does not choose Jesus will spend eternity with the devil.

The devil, who deceived them, was cast into the lake of fire and brimstone where the beast and the false prophet are. And they will be tormented day and night forever and ever. (Revelation 20:10)

Sometimes I have to stop and ask—do I dislike that person so much that I would have them thrown into the lake of fire where they are tormented day and night forever?

"If someone is committing all kinds of sins such as stealing, adultery, murder, or whatever, there is still only one thing that will send them into eternal damnation."

People often ask why the Lord doesn't just save everybody and wrap this whole thing up. I have a couple of answers to this. First, He wants people to freely choose to worship Him because they love Him. Second, He has given us that job to make disciples of all nations. God is not a God of force. Jesus was a gentleman and never forced His way into people lives. The Holy Spirit is also a gentleman who will not come into someone unless asked. All of them operate in love. He has called us to use His authority to bring in the harvest of souls—and get those other 2.4 billion Christians activated to pray, speak, and act.

For the god of this world has blinded the unbelievers' minds [that they should not discern the truth], preventing them from seeing the illuminating light of the Gospel of the glory of Christ (the Messiah), Who is the Image and Likeness of God. (II Corinthians 4:4 AMPC)

Step Two: Loose the Holy Spirit

Since the people we are praying for are blinded, we bind the blinders off of them so they have the opportunity to see. Then, we loose the Holy Spirit to enter into their lives and convict them of sin. Again, that sin is unbelief.

WISDOM FROM VICKI

The Holy Spirit knows each person intimately just like the Father knows each person intimately.

> *When you pray, don't babble on and on as the Gentiles do. They think their prayers are answered merely by repeating their words again and again. Don't be like them, for your Father knows exactly what you need even before you ask him!* (Matthew 6:7–8 NLT)

He wants us to ask based upon our intimate relationship. It's a conversation where He reveals His desire for you and the person you are praying for. The Holy Spirit is our personal Helper, guide, instructor, teacher, and advocate to lead us into all truth. One of His roles is to help you bring people to the Lord.

A Sample Prayer

Couple this with prayer binding the enemy off of them.

Father, in the name of Jesus, I loose the Holy Spirit into life, to convict them of the sin of not knowing Jesus as their Lord and Savior. I give the Holy Spirit free rein in their life to do whatever it takes to bring them into the knowledge of You in Jesus's name.

Chapter 6

Step Three:
Send Laborers

had the opportunity to travel to Japan several times. The population in Japan is overwhelmingly Shinto and Buddhist with a small sliver of Christianity. Japanese is the predominant language, but some of the younger people have been taught to speak English as a secondary language. Like Singapore, it's a great place to shop if you can afford it, and I feel completely safe there.

I love the Japanese people and culture but have discovered an immense pressure on them to succeed, which leads to high rates of alcoholism and suicide. I saw several people in meetings down a bottle of liquor after business discussions just to let loose. Because of so much pressure to operate flawlessly, saki, whiskey, or other liquors are consumed fast to numb the pain. They commit to things out of a deep sense of moral obligation—and they hate to disappoint.

In April 2023, the Japanese government initiated the Minister of Loneliness to tackle a major health crisis caused by increasing isolation and elevated suicide rates. I would not want that title, but I fell in love with the Japanese people.

One of their popular festivals involves walking through what they called a "holy" smoke bath. This is a Shinto practice intended to gain the devotee divine power and favor. They believe that fanning the smoke over themselves will bring healing or good fortune. I was asked to participate but told them I was already blessed, so I didn't need that. I'm not sure how that translated but it appeared to be okay. People do all kinds of ceremonies all over the world, but it does not reduce the loneliness because they do not have a relationship with the Lord Jesus.

LABORERS

The relationships available to us extend way beyond what people currently think. Seeing each member of the Body of Christ as a potential laborer can transform your life and the lives of others. Many people are introduced to the Lord through someone who comes into their sphere either as a short-term or long-term acquaintances. One of the challenges for all believers is to be a mentor beginning from the initial introduction and casual conversation. Every day, there are people coming into our orbit. We don't know where they are headed or any of their life decisions thus far. Sometimes, the best start is just to take the time to strike up a conversation. People like to talk. Laborers are those who actively look to engage even though they don't know where it will end up. When I just open it up to them, I listen for what is important to them and try to remember it for the next time.

Step Three: Send Laborers

Laborers are rewarded.

For the kingdom of heaven is like a landowner who went out early in the morning to hire laborers for his vineyard. Now when he had agreed with the laborers for a denarius a day, he sent them into his vineyard. And he went out about the third hour and saw others standing idle in the marketplace, and said to them, "You also go into the vineyard, and whatever is right I will give you." So they went. Again he went out about the sixth and the ninth hour, and did likewise. And about the eleventh hour he went out and found others standing idle, and said to them, "Why have you been standing here idle all day?" They said to him, "Because no one hired us." He said to them, "You also go into the vineyard, and whatever is right you will receive."

So when evening had come, the owner of the vineyard said to his steward, "Call the laborers and give them their wages, beginning with the last to the first." And when those came who were hired about the eleventh hour, they each received a denarius. But when the first came, they supposed that they would receive more; and they likewise received each a denarius. And when they had received it, they complained against the landowner, saying, "These last men have worked only one hour, and you made them equal to us who have borne the burden and the heat of the day." But he answered one of them and said, "Friend, I am doing you no wrong. Did you not agree with me for a denarius? Take what is yours and go your way. I wish to give to this last man the same

*as to you. Is it not lawful for me to do what I wish with
my own things? Or is your eye evil because I am good?"
So the last will be first, and the first last. For many are
called, but few chosen.* (Matthew 20:1–16)

Jesus told this story and called it an example of the kingdom.
It is about economics, but it is also about rewards. God is not
slack about rewarding people in this life and in heaven who
are obedient to what He wants accomplished.

*But without faith it is impossible to please Him, for he
who comes to God must believe that He is, and that He is
a rewarder of those who diligently seek Him.* (Hebrews
11:6)

Part of diligently seeking includes doing what He says—engaging in conversations to open the opportunity to share the
Good News. Part of the reward is God's peace and wisdom,
but the Lord will also compensate for time spent. Many times,
I have said, "Lord, I need to get this done quickly," referring to
some project, and He not only expedites it for me but we finish
with superior results! He more than makes up the difference.

During conversations, I often call on Him, asking for
words and insights that will impact that person and their life.
He knows the person I am speaking with inside and out; I
don't, yet, here we are conversing.

*Now therefore, go, and I will be with your mouth and
teach you what you shall say.* (Exodus 4:12)

If you ask and trust Him, handing over control of your
mouth, He will give you insight and words to say that will hit

His mark and achieve everything He intended through your conversation.

Churches overcomplicate this with door-to-door knocking, waiting to see if the person will open the door to discuss their potential heavenly destination. I'm not knocking the approach because I have participated in this as well. Those who actually open the door may say any number of things, savory or otherwise. It can be daunting for anyone starting out to read a script or respond appropriately as people react. I could go off into a lot of shock value stories, but that would turn this book from G-rated to R-rated quickly. At the end of any adventure like that, you do reach people that may not be reached by other people, but it is not the only way.

"If you ask and trust Him, handing over control of your mouth, He will give you insight and words to say that will hit His mark and achieve everything He intended through your conversation."

Jesus went into synagogues (churches), the marketplaces, and joined people in their homes when invited. He gathered people around Him, teaching and preaching, but He also chose people to train. He started with twelve and then ordained the additional seventy disciples (Luke 10), sending them out ahead of Him.

He was saying to them, "The harvest is abundant [for there are many who need to hear the good news about salvation], but the workers [those available to proclaim the message of salvation] are few. Therefore, [prayerfully] ask the Lord of the harvest to send out workers into His harvest." (Luke 10:2 AMP)

Why does He instruct us to pray and ask the Lord to send workers/laborers into the harvest field? If God wants those people to come into a relationship with Him, why doesn't He snap His fingers and make it happen?

When you pray what Jesus has said, you are praying His perfect will. Your own heart comes into alignment making you closer to and more like Him. In speaking and praying His heart, you are using your earthly authority to give Him permission to motivate, move, and even supernaturally "translate" people to get the job done.

In some situations, although you have tried many times, there may be others that a person will more readily listen to. I have on occasions tried to have spiritual discussions about spiritual subjects with members of my own family only to have seemingly no impact. Then, one of their friends will come along saying the same thing and they respond, "Wow! That is great!"

Don't get upset—just be thankful they heard!

God is love and has a sense of humor. If you enable Him to motivate laborers, including you, then stand back and see what great things the Lord will do.

Now an angel of the Lord spoke to Philip, saying, "Arise and go toward the south along the road which goes down from Jerusalem to Gaza." This is desert. So he arose and went. And behold, a man of Ethiopia, a eunuch of great authority under Candace the queen of the Ethiopians, who had charge of all her treasury, and had come to Jerusalem to worship, was returning. And sitting in his chariot, he was reading Isaiah the prophet. Then the Spirit said to Philip, "Go near and overtake this chariot." So Philip ran to him, and heard him reading the prophet Isaiah, and said, "Do you understand what you are reading?" And he said, "How can I, unless someone guides me?" And he asked Philip to come up and sit with him. The place in the Scripture which he read was this: "He was led as a sheep to the slaughter; And as a lamb before its shearer is silent, So He opened not His mouth. In His humiliation His justice was taken away, and who will declare His generation? For His life is taken from the earth." So the eunuch answered Philip and said, "I ask you, of whom does the prophet say this, of himself or of some other man?" Then Philip opened his mouth, and beginning at this Scripture, preached Jesus to him. Now as they went down the road, they came to some water. And the eunuch said, "See, here is water. What hinders me from being baptized?" Then Philip said, "If you believe with all your heart, you may." And he answered and said, "I believe that Jesus Christ is the Son of God." So he commanded the chariot to stand still. And both Philip and the eunuch went down into the water, and he baptized him.

When they came up out of the water, the Spirit of the Lord [suddenly] took Philip [and carried him] away [to a different place]; and the eunuch no longer saw him,

*but he went on his way rejoicing. But Philip found him-
self at Azotus, and as he passed through he preached the
good news [of salvation] to all the cities, until he came
to Caesarea [Maritima].* (Acts 8:26–38 NKJV; 39–40
AMP)

We start this passage with Philip going out of his way for some
yet undisclosed divine appointment. As the eunuch entered
the scene, Philip realized he was there to inform, convert, and
baptize the man God sent him to meet. Then, in an instant,
Philip was suddenly "carried" away to another location to
preach the Good News.

It takes all kinds of people to reach all kinds of people. We
just have to be willing and available. If you give the Lord permission, He can cause others to go out of their way to come
across people you are praying for. You be willing to labor for
the people God sends along your path and He will send others out of their way to labor for your family.

LONELINESS EPIDEMIC

Loneliness is widespread not only in Japan, but globally. In
May 2023, the U.S. also declared a health emergency related
to loneliness and lack of social connection. That is partly why
people seek an identity in social media. Social media affords
us a shallow opportunity to portray ourselves as someone of
significance. People are yearning for conversation, but they
don't know how to obtain it. Even some psychologists have
recommended that society return to church where they can
find community. Be willing to reach out to people to have
conversations and start the process toward their salvation.

Step Three: Send Laborers

Recently, I heard a story about a woman the Lord was pressing to attend a tattoo convention. The intention was to start conversations with people by offering to interpret their dreams and tattoos but, in her own mind, she had nothing in common with the people attending this convention. Like many of us, she would have preferred not to go.

She went anyway.

The first person she encountered was a pastor's daughter who had been estranged from her father and from her faith, but who wanted a tattoo interpretation. Wow! What a great inroad into that person's life! It gave the initially unwilling laborer the opportunity to lead someone else's daughter to the Good News. Her obedience made her the answer to someone else's prayers.

There are so many out there searching for identity and significance. They may look strange to us or show every sign of not wanting to communicate. My favorite is when people stare at their phone. Sometimes we just need to buy them coffee, sit back, and let them talk, being ready and willing to carefully guide the conversation to the Lord.

"People are yearning for conversation."

You can never be sure where someone is along their process of coming to Jesus. The Good News metaphorically compares this to an agricultural process.

Who then is Paul, and who is Apollos, but ministers through whom you believed, as the Lord gave to each one? I planted, Apollos watered, but God gave the increase. So then neither he who plants is anything, nor he who waters, but God who gives the increase. Now he who plants and he who waters are one, and each one will receive his own reward according to his own labor. For we are God's fellow workers; you are God's field, you are God's building. According to the grace of God which was given to me, as a wise master builder I have laid the foundation, and another builds on it. But let each one take heed how he builds on it. For no other foundation can anyone lay than that which is laid, which is Jesus Christ. (I Corinthians 3:5–11)

If we do our part, God will get the glory, but we will receive a reward as if we had led them to the Lord.

DISCUSSION SUGGESTIONS

I used to be terrible at starting up conversations. I would rather stand in the corner and stare at everybody or stay at home. I am a work in progress on the social scale.

My wife is extremely gifted at that. I tried to pay her one time to just go in my place, hand out business cards, and do whatever needed to be done, but she laughed when I offered her money and, of course, said, "No."

I do get exhausted when chatting with people for over an hour, but I'm getting better.

As a believer, you should always be looking for inroads into people's lives through conversations. I typically start out looking for their interests. Once we hit the right topic, they open up and do most of the talking. Whether the discussion is about their business, computer games, sports, hunting, fishing, kids, or grandkids, I try to find the subject they really enjoy. Some people may not be interested in talking at all, which can be frustrating. Just don't get pushy. It may take a little fishing to find something they want to engage.

Allowing the Lord to speak through you can be challenging. Just remind yourself that the Lord knows them intimately and He can say things to them through you that cut through all of the blockades. It's like the young pastor's daughter at a tattoo convention—one person prayed, and another did the talking, and the Lord brought the harvest.

> *Live wisely among those who are not believers and make the most of every opportunity. Let your conversation be gracious and attractive so that you will have the right response for everyone.* (Colossians 4:5–6 NLT)

The right response is whatever the Lord wants you to say. Sometimes we look for the perfect answer, but the Lord just wants to let them know that He knows them, He loves them, and He wants them closer to Him!

When I am at church, I look for people who are standing off by themselves and introduce myself. Just because they are in church does not mean they have a relationship with the Lord. They may just be there in a desperate cry to get their life together, or for a myriad of other reasons. Having done this many times, I have found that most people have problems they are dealing with and they are coming to church looking for answers. That's good! As we converse, they may mention marriage issues, health challenges, loneliness—there are so many hurts and needs. If they do share something that's weighing on them, you can offer to pray with them about it. I try to pray with them right there lest I forget or miss the opportunity. I have never been turned down, even with what appeared to be the hardest-hearted person.

"As a believer, you should always be looking for inroads into people's lives through conversation."

WISDOM FROM VICKI

Are they not all ministering spirits sent forth to minister for those who will inherit salvation? (Hebrews 1:14)

Among the laborers we don't get to visibly see are angels. They are here for our assistance. In Acts 8:26 mentioned earlier, it was an angel who instructed Philip to go to a certain place to lead someone to salvation. The angel was instructed to tell Philip to be there. God can get the right laborers to the right place at the right time with the right words to say because people were praying.

In Acts 10:3, an angel spoke to Cornelius. He was led to the Lord because prayers were going up from his household to the God of Israel.

And they said, "Cornelius the centurion, a just man, one who fears God and has a good reputation among all the nation of the Jews, was divinely instructed by a holy angel to summon you to his house, and to hear words from you." (Acts 10:22)

Step Three: Send Laborers

When sending laborers, send your angels to round them up and get them in the right place at the right time. The Holy Spirit will provide them with the words to say.

A laborer is one who helps bring in the harvest. Jesus taught His disciples—us—to be a light and to so shine that others would be drawn to us. It helps to have something to say when asked why you look so peaceful and happy. Think through your testimony, especially the parts you feel will be most impactful. This insight will emerge as you listen closely to what the person is saying, all the while asking the Lord to reveal anything you can touch on that will impact their life.

People don't necessarily tell you what is going on. I may pray for what they ask but I'm also simultaneously asking the Holy Spirit to direct my words in such a powerful way as to reveal the truth—not for their amazement, but so they realize that the God of the universe knows them and wants a personal relationship with them.

A Sample Prayer

Father, in Jesus's name, I know You desire all people to be saved and come to knowledge of the truth. Concerning _____, I pray in accordance with Your Word that You send laborers across their path to ultimately bring them into relationship with You. I also call upon the angels to work in conjunction with laborers who've been chosen and picked out for _____. Let Your laborers be in the right place at the right time with the right words to say. In Jesus's name, I give You permission to do what it takes to lead them into acceptance of Jesus as their Lord and Savior.

I always like to add, "Do what it takes to bring them in," because some people are more stubborn than others. You are giving the Lord and the angels permission to do whatever it takes, meaning, "Don't leave them alone until they accept You as Lord and Savior!"

Chapter 7

Step Four:
Open Hearts to
Hear the Good News

On two occasions I was in Kazakhstan, which used to be part of the Soviet Union. Kazakhstan's claim to fame is their direct descendancy to Genghis Khan. This is the first and only place I'm aware of where horse meat was the staple diet. Most of the people speak Russian but there is also a Kazakh language. No one spoke English except for the interpreter—this is when you pray the interpreter knows English well and will be able to pick up at least most of what you're putting down.

For those who don't remember or didn't know, the Soviet Union was anti-God and really did not tolerate religions. I had the opportunity to travel through parts of the country and observe the local life, especially in the countryside. Kazakhstan was also one of the states where the Soviet Union used to test nuclear bombs, a sobering fact I was once reminded of as I rode past a facility that was condemned due to radiation.

The spiritual environment at the time was control and distrust.

The people are currently 70 percent Muslim. The rest are mostly what is called Eastern Orthodox (or Russian Orthodox). From what I could gather, the Eastern Orthodox church at one time acted as an informant to the Soviet Union identifying people illegally practicing religion, so there was a widespread social distrust of organized religions.

My hotel room overlooked the local mosque. It was an extremely quiet hotel. While I was working in the room, I decided to turn on the TV to at least create some noise. There were no strong internet signals there yet. All the channels were either in Kazakh or Russian except for one English speaking channel—CNN.

CNN was talking about the state of the U.S. economy and commenting on how bad it was. The last thing I heard before I turned it off was, "If you think that it is bad, it's going to get really bad."

"The fewer people who suffer damage—either from direct injury, emotional duress, or reputational damage—the less damage your organization will suffer."

Step Four: Open Hearts to Hear the Good News

EARS MADE TO HEAR

Our ears are made to hear things even if it is background noise. Fear can build up quickly if you start hearing bad reports, whether true or not. There are times when I just have to shut things off because of negative reports. Am I in denial?

This is free will. We can choose to walk down the path of fear or faith. We have the ability to take things that we see, hear, and think, and bring them into our hearts. The Good News refers to this as meditating. Meditating is thinking and saying words or ideas of Scripture over and over until we get them inside us and start projecting them in our life.

> *For You formed my inward parts; You covered me in my mother's womb. I will praise You, for I am fearfully and wonderfully made; marvelous are Your works, and that my soul knows very well. My frame was not hidden from You, when I was made in secret, and skillfully wrought in the lowest parts of the earth. Your eyes saw my substance, being yet unformed. And in Your book they all were written, the days fashioned for me, when as yet there were none of them.* (Psalm 139:13–16)

Every person born into this world is fearfully and wonderfully made. God gave them a spirit, a soul, and a body. The soul is typically referred to as our mind, will, and emotions. He has given us the ability to think, apply logic, and sense God's presence. He has also given us the ability to hear.

When we are born again, He gives us the ability to walk like Jesus in every way by His Spirit. When the Good News refers to the heart, it is talking about the spiritual heart where our emotions and desires dwell. The heart is the center of our

101

universe in which we hear God and from which we make decisions.

> *And on the Sabbath day we went out of the city to the riverside, where prayer was customarily made; and we sat down and spoke to the women who met there. Now a certain woman named Lydia heard us. She was a seller of purple from the city of Thyatira, who worshiped God. The Lord opened her heart to heed the things spoken by Paul. And when she and her household were baptized, she begged us, saying, "If you have judged me to be faithful to the Lord, come to my house and stay." So she persuaded us.* (Acts 16:13–15)

The Lord "opened her heart" to hear what was being spoken by Paul. We can hear a lot of things on any given day, but there are some things that will create a life-altering path.

> *How then shall they call on Him in whom they have not believed? And how shall they believe in Him of whom they have not heard? And how shall they hear without a preacher? And how shall they preach unless they are sent? As it is written: "How beautiful are the feet of those who preach the gospel of peace, who bring glad tidings of good things!"* (Romans 10:14–15)

We often get caught up thinking we need to hire or call upon a professional preacher. I don't mean to downplay people coming to church, but any one of us can tell others the Good News and expect the same results. Paul is talking about "regular" people like you and me speaking and preaching the Good News. There are unsaved masses listening to the radio, watching podcasts, or sitting in restaurants hearing whatever is playing in the background. These are opportunities for people to hear a message or be engaged in conversations even though they are outside the four walls of a church building, or in any number of spaces that don't look like a place to preach the Good News. In the case of Lydia, the Lord opened her heart to hear Paul preach "where prayer was customarily made."

> *"Therefore let all the house of Israel know assuredly that God has made this Jesus, whom you crucified, both Lord and Christ." Now when they heard this, they were cut to the heart, and said to Peter and the rest of the apostles, "Men and brethren, what shall we do?" Then Peter said to them, "Repent, and let every one of you be baptized in the name of Jesus Christ for the remission of sins; and you shall receive the gift of the Holy Spirit."* (Acts 2:36–38)

The Good News used the expression "cut to the heart." Their hearts were opened to hear the Word concerning Christ and it "cut," meaning pricked, stung, and pierced. It's the difference between vaguely hearing background noise and the Holy Spirit gaining permission to access the heart and upheave someone's life for the good. The hearers were boldly confronted with the truth and had a decision to make. They could have walked away thinking it was idle chatter but they did not. The truth is the Word, and the Word is a sword. They heard the truth and it pierced, impacting them so much that they had to stop and ask, "What must we do?" Thankfully, there was someone there with the answer.

No matter the country or environment, asking the Lord to open people's ears to hear the truth can cause the right person to dominate the airwaves.

"He can cause people to hear His call to salvation in the midst of anything."

WISDOM FROM VICKI

The Lord does not want us to be ignorant. In the words of Jesus:

> *To you it has been given to know the mysteries of the kingdom of God, but to the rest it is given in parables, that "Seeing they may not see, and hearing they may not understand." … For nothing is secret that will not be revealed, nor anything hidden that will not be known and come to light.* (Luke 8:10, 17)

When I ask the Lord questions, I am expecting with biblical hope to get an answer. His response may come during a church service, a radio or television program, a podcast, or conversations. I'm always amazed when the Lord answers me in the midst of much noise. Part of wisdom is seeking Him for answers—and He is faithful to provide them. In the middle of all the noise, wisdom is flowing. He can cause people to hear His call to salvation in the midst of anything.

A Sample Prayer

Father, in Jesus's name, I ask that, by the power of the Holy Spirit, You open up _____ heart to the Good News being preached, no matter what the method. Along with laborers I

Step Four: Open Hearts to Hear the Good News

command all channels of hearing to be activated so that they hear and come into the knowledge of the truth.

Chapter 8

Step Five:
Speak in Agreement
with Your Prayer

I was fortunate to travel into Brazil with a native Portuguese speaker. I stayed as close to him as I possibly could.

Brazil is heavily Roman Catholic but evangelistic churches have also risen up over the past few years. There is a heavy spirit of corruption in Brazil that permeates from the government on down into all parts of society. On the good side, the food is great.

My traveling companion told me that if I went into certain areas, he could guarantee that I would be shot with no questions asked. Since we started in Rio, I wanted to go out and see what Rio was like at night but he guaranteed me that I would at best be mugged, but only if I was lucky. Once again—back to the hotel room to read and pray.

On the first trip, we flew to different industrial cities to understand what each area could offer. On the second, he drove me through the countryside from Rio to Macau. I saw a lot of low-income farms and low-income properties. It requires no skill and no faith to just start calling things like they are and justify the vast corruption as being hopeless—but God!

"It requires no skill and no fatih to just start calling things like they are and justify the vast corruption as being hopeless—but God!"

KEEP OUR CONFESSIONS LINED UP

Once we start praying for someone, it can be easy to contradict our own prayers because of something they say or do. During holidays or birthdays, on social media, or anywhere people gather, a person's behaviors may show up as contrary to what we saw in God's heart and can tempt us to give up. The Good News does not mince words about this. When we doubt what God has said, James calls us "doubleminded" and warns that we should expect to receive nothing from God:

> *If any of you lacks wisdom, let him ask of God, who gives to all liberally and without reproach, and it will be given to him. But let him ask in faith, with no doubting, for he who doubts is like a wave of the sea driven and tossed by the wind. **For let not that man suppose that he will receive anything from the Lord; he is a double-minded man,** unstable in all his ways.* (James 1:5–8, emphasis mine)

Step Five: Speak in Agreement with Your Prayer

The waves of the sea "driven and tossed by the wind" refers to opinions that quickly shift from one position to another, especially based on what we see and hear. We might even find ourselves looking at all the bad things a person has done and say, "I don't see how that person could ever be saved." We have all done this from time to time.

It is most difficult with people we know and love. I will repeat this point again: when you are praying for someone and all hell starts coming to the surface in them, you know you are right over the target. The demonic realm is trying to offend and knock us off track. As the Good News teaches, we overcome Satan's evil schemes by walking in forgiveness:

> *When you forgive this man, I forgive him, too. And when I forgive whatever needs to be forgiven, I do so with Christ's authority for your benefit, so that Satan will not outsmart us. For we are familiar with his evil schemes.* (II Corinthians 2:10–11 NLT)

If someone starts chewing you out while you're praying for them, don't take it personally. Understand it is an evil scheme launched by the demonic realm to distract you. Believe me, I have been chewed out and insulted by the best of them. The demonic realm launches schemes to keep people from coming into a saving knowledge of Jesus. If we take the bait, we delay the efforts.

> *Don't you see how wonderfully kind, tolerant, and patient God is with you? Does this mean nothing to you? Can't you see that his kindness is intended to turn you from your sin?* (Romans 2:4 NLT)

Repentance is a gift from God where He gives us the opportunity to get ourselves back on God's side. It means admitting we made a mistake and returning to the right course. No matter how bad things appear to be or how hard it may feel to believe the person can be saved, their repentance can completely transform them and their situation. I liken it to a forgiven do-over that you learn from. For the people that play golf, it is like a mulligan—only this is a divine do-over. Their shot doesn't count, so now they go at it again like there was never a mistake—and the same is true for us if we have temporarily fallen prey to doubt. But holding on to an offense is rooted in unforgiveness and will cause our words to line up with the offense. It can even change what we believe about God's willingness and ability to answer our prayers. Jesus instructed us:

> So Jesus answered and said to them, "Have faith in God. For assuredly, I say to you, whoever says to this mountain, 'Be removed and be cast into the sea,' and does not doubt in his heart, but believes that those things he says will be done, he will have whatever he says. **Therefore I say to you, whatever things you ask when you pray, believe that you receive them, and you will have them.** And whenever you stand praying, if you have anything against anyone, forgive him, that your Father in heaven may also forgive you your trespasses. But if you do not forgive, neither will your Father in heaven forgive your trespasses." (Mark 11:22–26, emphasis mine)

In order to be truly effective in the kingdom of God, forgiveness has to happen quickly. I have a litmus test to determine whether I truly believe that I have received what I prayed. It's not based on how great my prayer was but whether my words concerning that person continue to line up with my prayer for them.

Every person's heart is impacted by what we hear, see, and speak. If we say what the Good News says consistently enough, our spirit lines up with our mouth and we align with the Word. Every time we say, "That person is saved," it builds faith in us. This takes practice. When we blow it and speak in agreement with Satan, the accuser, our failure does not have to be permanent. God is so gracious to give us the gift of repentance—the ability to change our course by simply saying, "I was wrong." Repent and quickly realign your words with what you prayed: "This person is saved and walking in the knowledge of the truth."

"In order to be truely effective in the kingdom of God, forgiveness has to happen quickly."

In the same breath that Jesus says to believe that you have received your prayer, He also says, "And whenever you stand praying, if you have anything against anyone, forgive him." Walking in forgiveness is a full-time job. It takes discipline to stop, repent, and get back on track with your Good News confessions. Let nothing come between you and the people God has placed on your heart; but if you are holding any unforgiveness against them, quickly repent. You may have to do this multiple times in one day. Jesus will accept your repentance as many times it takes.

Give all your worries and cares to God, for he cares about you. Stay alert! Watch out for your great enemy, the devil. He prowls around like a roaring lion, looking for someone to devour. Stand firm against him and be strong in your faith. (I Peter 5:7–9 NLT)

The roaring lion is the one making the loudest noise. When you pray for people, you may expect them to glow and look back at you lovingly and grateful for your service but instead you find you just woke up a hungry, roaring lion. Walk in forgiveness of that person screaming at you. Stay alert and know what is happening. Standing firm against "your great enemy, the devil" means being strong in faith and offering forgiveness on every level so that we see our prayers answered.

Growing up playing sports, the most powerful football plays were not the fancy unexpected ones but basic diversion tactics—start to run the ball to the right and then suddenly pivot left. The devil tries to get us to look right and then look left. He wants to get our attention off what God is showing us so he can steal the opportunity for us and the person we are praying for. It is called distraction.

Being alert and refusing to take the bait is part of the battle. Walking in forgiveness is a vital component of our victory.

WISDOM FROM VICKI

It helps to go over my confessions daily as part of my prayer time. Sometimes, when I have to jump in the car to hurry towards a commitment, I use the drive as my prayer time. It helps keep me positive no matter what someone is saying or doing to me so that the battle is won and that person comes into the saving knowledge of Jesus. Repeating my confessions keeps me from being double-minded.

If we speak our confessions enough, we will find that the truth effortlessly flows out from our innermost being when we and others need it the most.

> *Love is patient and kind. Love is not jealous or boastful or proud or rude. It does not demand its own way. It is not irritable, and it keeps no record of being wronged.* (I Corinthians 13:4–5 NLT)

Love does not hold onto a suffered wrong. Love is not touchy, fearful, or resentful but "patient and kind." Love never fails.

It's not always easy to forgive, especially if someone gets on your nerves and you're around them often, but people take notice when you choose to love rather than mirror others' poor behavior. Your love will eventually wear them down. It is the strongest spiritual force in the universe.

Sample Sayings

Isaiah 54:13 – All my children are taught by the Lord and great shall be the peace of my children.

I Timothey 2:4 – My desire and prayer is that _____ is saved and comes to the knowledge of the truth.

Acts 11:14 – My desire is for _____ to receive the words by which they and all their household will be saved.

For the Jewish person:

Romans 9:27 – Though the number of the children of Israel be as the sand of the sea, the remnant _____ are saved.

Chapter 9

Step Six:
Praise the Lord in Advance

A friend of mine was with the Secret Service tasked to protect U.S. dignitaries while traveling. Occasionally, he would ask about my upcoming trips and then offer any insights he might have about the place. This time, I told him I was going to Cartagena, Colombia, and he chuckled. Cartegena is where the Colombian cartels reside. His advice: "Keep your head low and don't draw attention to yourself."

Colombia is heavily old Roman Catholic, but evangelical Christian churches have risen up over the years. The spiritual climate in Colombia has been one of fear and control.

Travel can be joyful or grueling depending upon those "incidentals," the things that happen that you couldn't anticipate and would never plan for. I had tried to coordinate this trip with another traveler so I didn't have to be alone but that didn't work out. So, here I was, heading for a country I had never been to with no one I knew.

First, I flew into Bogotá and needed to find my connecting flight but it was in a different terminal. Then, my second misfortune—no one spoke English, only Spanish. I found a merciful person who uttered what sounded like a terminal name and then told me to walk "that way." By the grace of God, I found the right terminal and the right flight.

Flying into Cartegena and landing by yourself in the middle of the night can be unnerving, to say the least. I soon discovered that no one in this airport spoke English either. At the time of my visit, Colombia was also known as the kidnapping capital of the world. Oh, the things you think about when you travel. I learned to be flexible and aware of my surroundings.

I got into a taxi and did my best to explain to the driver where I was going. He took off. Once outside the city, there were zero lights and no cell phone signals. My mind raced—this could be it. I may never be seen again. The driver made a big sudden U-turn in the narrow road and pointed at some lights in the distance. Thank God! It was my hotel.

I was booked in a luxury room on the second floor. The doors didn't offer much soundproofing. Whatever was in the jungle out there would easily get through and I occasionally heard someone scream from the first floor. The bed was a brick bed with a mattress on top. Oh well, so much for sleep. Who needs that?

On the trip back, every plane in existence seemingly broke down. I had to stay a couple of extra days until another plane could be put into service.

Whether it is Brazil, Canada, Colombia, Honduras, Nicaragua, or the United States, there will be demonic attacks to keep you focused on weird things and great opportunities to get angry at whatever is happening around you—rather than praying for those countries. If you let it, your mind will race until you can find nothing but bad things popping into your mind. Sometimes you just have to start praising God before you punch somebody. It may just start with, "Praise the Lord!" If that's what you have, then say, "Praise the Lord!" as many times as you need to. As you start your mind and words in that direction, you will begin to sense the presence of God.

"The Lord can get more done while we are busy with praising Him than we can do by ourselves with all of our busy efforts combined."

PRAISE CONFOUNDS THE ENEMY

God likes for His people to praise Him, especially when you want to do the opposite. Praise, thanksgiving, and giving God glory in the face of stern opposition tends to confuse your adversary, the devil.

Second Chronicles 20 tells the story of a great army from Ammon coming against Jerusalem. The army was massive and there appeared to be no hope.

The devil always tries to play his "massive, overwhelming odds card" to make people feel overwhelmed, but the king at that time, whose name was Jehoshaphat, went before the Lord to hear what his next steps should be. Then a word from the Lord came to him from a prophet:

You will not need to fight in this battle. Position your-
selves, stand still and see the salvation of the Lord, who
is with you, O Judah and Jerusalem! Do not fear or be
dismayed; tomorrow go out against them, for the LORD
is with you. (II Chronicles 20:17)

Jehoshaphat and the prophet told the people the Lord's in-
structions— the worshipers must go ahead of the army and
praise the Lord.

After consulting the people, the king appointed singers to
walk ahead of the army, singing to the LORD and prais-
ing him for his holy splendor. This is what they sang:
"Give thanks to the LORD; his faithful love endures for-
ever!" At the very moment they began to sing and give
praise, the LORD caused the armies of Ammon, Moab,
and Mount Seir to start fighting among themselves. The
armies of Moab and Ammon turned against their al-
lies from Mount Seir and killed every one of them. After
they had destroyed the army of Seir, they began attack-
ing each other. (II Chronicles 20:21–23 NLT)

One of the amazing things that comes out of praise is wisdom.
You praise and God tells you what to do. He might give you
a slight course correction or you may hear those comforting
words, "I've got this." The Lord can get more done while we
are busy with praising Him than we can do by ourselves with
all of our busy efforts combined.

Israel's praise brought confusion to the enemy and they
began to turn on each other. When we praise the Lord in the
middle of immense pressure and where things look hopeless,

Step Six: Praise the Lord in Advance

God can intervene on our behalf and bring the victory. When people worship the Lord, our enemies flee.

In Acts 13 there was a meeting in Antioch to discuss and plan the way forward. They began worshiping and praising the Lord.

> *Among the prophets and teachers of the church at Antioch of Syria were Barnabas, Simeon (called "the black man"), Lucius (from Cyrene), Manaen (the childhood companion of King Herod Antipas), and Saul. One day as these men were worshiping the Lord and fasting, the Holy Spirit said, "Appoint Barnabas and Saul for the special work to which I have called them." So after more fasting and prayer, the men laid their hands on them and sent them on their way.* (Acts 13:1–3 NLT)

Once again, they worshiped the Lord and the Spirit of the Lord told them what to do. Worship can be spoken or sung. When we are at an impasse or the pressure from the demonic realm gets intense, praise is a key to victory. In praise, we understand that we have reached the end of what our efforts can accomplish and are reaching into God to receive affirmation, remove confusion, or run off demonic spirits.

The New Testament refers to singing psalms, hymns, and spiritual songs with thanksgiving. The way to get God involved is to sing with thankfulness.

> *Let the message about Christ, in all its richness, fill your lives. Teach and counsel each other with all the wisdom he gives. Sing psalms and hymns and spiritual songs to God with thankful hearts. And whatever you do or say, do it as a representative of the Lord Jesus, giving thanks*

through him to God the Father. (Colossians 3:16–17 NLT)

The Amplified translation says it this way:

Let the [spoken] word of Christ have its home within you [dwelling in your heart and mind—permeating every aspect of your being] as you teach [spiritual things] and admonish and train one another with all wisdom, singing psalms and hymns and spiritual songs with thankfulness in your hearts to God.

God loves when His people sing praises to Him—even and especially when we don't feel like it. Whether we are praising from the Scriptures or singing and speaking in our own words with thankful hearts, God will intervene on our behalf. When you praise Him for a person's salvation even though they just screamed at you, you will run demonic spirits off as God brings conviction of their sin. Our spiritual father of the faith, Abraham, set the example:

*He did not waver at the promise of God through unbelief, but was strengthened in faith, **giving glory to God**, and being fully convinced that what He had promised He was also able to perform.* (Romans 4:20–21, emphasis mine)

God said that the number of Abraham's descendants would be greater than the sands of the sea; yet, Abraham's wife, Sarah, was barren and they had both surpassed natural child-bearing years. Though having a child had become physically impossible, Abraham believed even in the midst of impossible circumstances and gave glory to God. What do you think that sounded like? I do not think he was quiet or modest as he gave glory to God for the child to come. If you waver based upon what you hear, see, or think about a person or their salvation, it's time to give glory to God, get wisdom, and run the devil off.

"When you praise Him for a person's salvation even though they just screamed at you, you will run demonic spirits off as God brings conviction of their sin."

THANKFULNESS

I sometimes have to practice thankfulness. It's easy to whine about things going the wrong direction, but putting on a thankful heart, simply saying, "I thank You, Lord, that I am saved!" kickstarts a reversal of heart from being full of whining to full of true gratitude. I may have to say the same words of thanks several times just to start turning that wheel in the right direction, but then the Lord helps me. He reminds me of all the times He graciously pulled me out of troubles. He meets me in the space of praise, causing the thoughts of my heart to accelerate in gratitude while the misery of whining and complaining vanishes.

On the other hand, there may be times when we've dug a hole too deep, practicing and rehearsing our ingratitude. The longer that goes on, the more difficult it can be to turn our heart and return to a state of thankfulness. That's when I turn to the Psalms (I have already highlighted all the good parts) and speak the Scriptures that praise Him. His Word cuts the enemy to pieces and causes him to run.

Thanksgiving and thankfulness are major themes in Scripture because the Lord has done so much for us. Like any Father, He appreciates it when His children say thanks.

> *Rejoice always, pray without ceasing, in everything give thanks; for this is the will of God in Christ Jesus for you.* (I Thessalonians 5:16–18)

The Amplified Bible says it this way:

> *Rejoice always and delight in your faith; be unceasing and persistent in prayer; in every situation [no matter what the circumstances] be thankful and continually give thanks to God; for this is the will of God for you in Christ Jesus.*

"Delight in" means to celebrate your faith. Pray without ceasing like the persistent widow in Luke 18. No matter the circumstances, hardships, annoyances, or legitimate grievances—"in everything give thanks" to the Lord.

Someone you prayed for may have spat horrible words in your face or behind your back. Rejoice because the enemy is on the run and it won't be long before that person is saved. I often remind myself that He provided a way for all people to be saved. I am thankful for Jesus who saved me and for the people who prayed for me while I was lost and blind. And Christ not only saved us but He gave us His Holy Spirit to lead and guide and live inside us. By the Holy Spirit, the grace of God empowers us each and every day.

Step Six: Praise the Lord in Advance

When I meditate on the fact that I am saved and going to heaven and not bound for hell, and that I have opportunities to take others with me—WOW—my heart leaps!! He gave us a free will but He placed eternity in each of our hearts so we would search Him out.

> *So be careful how you live. Don't live like fools, but like those who are wise. Make the most of every opportunity in these evil days. Don't act thoughtlessly but understand what the Lord wants you to do. Don't be drunk with wine, because that will ruin your life. Instead, be filled with the Holy Spirit, singing psalms and hymns and spiritual songs among yourselves, and making music to the Lord in your hearts. And give thanks for everything to God the Father in the name of our Lord Jesus Christ.* (Ephesians 5:15–20 NLT)

"Don't live thoughtlessly but understand what the Lord wants you to do"—and when you're not sure, simply ask Him. Live wisely; make use of the time; be filled and overflowing with the Holy Spirit; sing spiritual songs; make music to the Lord in your heart; give thanks for everything. These crush depression and open avenues for the Lord to lead you more clearly and precisely.

Sometimes you just start with humming. Then, as you continue, it builds until you overflow into outright singing. Even in an oppressive environment you can throw a spiritual party. Even on a twenty-fourhour plane ride you can have a party just giving thanks to the Lord, for He is good and His mercies endure forever. Eventually, someone will ask, "Why are you so happy?" This is the open door to discuss our gracious, loving God! As the Scriptures repeatedly tell us:

And whatever you do in word or deed, do all in the name of the Lord Jesus, giving thanks to God the Father through Him. (Colossians 3:17)

When we practice thankfulness to God, we will see strongholds in people's lives crumble as we attract more people so we can share the Good News.

"Eventually, someone will ask, 'Why are you so happy?'"

WISDOM FROM VICKI

Before we get into this, God knows your voice is excellent, so cast off any concerns of turning off the Spirit of God by being off tune when you sing. Your greatest victories come from praising the Lord. His praises confound and scatter the enemy, which is the demonic realm.

Sometimes this can just start out with the sample praises below. Ultimately, the Lord loves for you to sing to Him in a free-flowing form of thanks and praise that comes right from your own heart.

But you are a chosen generation, a royal priesthood, a holy nation, His own special people, that you may proclaim the praises of Him who called you out of darkness into His marvelous light; who once were not a people but are now the people of God, who had not obtained mercy but now have obtained mercy. (I Peter 2:9–10)

Step Six: Praise the Lord in Advance

We praise Him because He delivered us out of darkness into His marvelous light—you just the same as the person you are praying for. As you praise Him, His presence begins to inhabit the situation.

> *You will show me the path of life; in Your presence is fullness of joy; at Your right hand are pleasures forevermore.* (Psalm 16:11)

I encourage you to always have a way to write down or record what you hear or experience as you turn to God to praise Him because encouraging words and direction often flow to you as you press in. And this is all part of building intimacy with Him.

Sample Praises

Lord, I praise You that You desire none be lost but all come into the saving knowledge of You.

Lord, I praise You that _____ is saved.

Lord, I praise You that _____ is serving You and reaching other people for the kingdom of God.

Lord, I praise You that my children are taught of the Lord and great is their peace.

Lord, I praise You that the seed of the righteous shall be delivered.

Chapter 10

Step Seven:
Disciple Them in the Word

've had the opportunity to travel to many international countries, but I need to talk about the United States, particularly Washington, D.C. D.C. is inhabited by spirits of power and prostitution, which inbreed corruption.

Once, I walked out of my hotel room to see the sights and get something to eat. To my right and to my left were homeless people and protestors potentially up to no good. I decided to stay inside the hotel and have all my meals there. Back to the room to read and pray. I eventually returned as a tourist with my wife.

Many fine politicians and businesspeople go to D.C. with righteous intentions but ultimately start voting or lobbying for positions they were not previously in favor of. We are quick to tag it as corruption, but there are spiritual forces that need to be dealt with. In the first chapter, we talked about praying for all people including kings and all in authority—from the school board to the president of our nation.

When you look at various kings in the Old Testament, the more corrupt the king, the more corrupt the king's country. As we discussed earlier, the more corrupt and power hungry the emperors or kings, the worse for the people and throughout society.

In the corporate world, if there is vileness with executive leadership, I can guarantee it is rolling through the organization. It is a good idea to go back and review chapter four, "Bind the Enemy Off of Their Minds," as you pray for people with a persistent spirit.

No matter what country I was in, I was always glad to get back into America.

MAKING DISCIPLES

Therefore, go and make disciples of all the nations, baptizing them in the name of the Father and the Son and the Holy Spirit. Teach these new disciples to obey all the commands I have given you. And be sure of this: I am with you always, even to the end of the age. (Matthew 28:19–20 NLT)

When talking about nations, Jesus is also referring to all people groups. Again, "all" means "all." Beyond being saved, we need to make sure they are baptized and that they understand all of Jesus's commands. It's easy for us to say, "That's the church's job," referring to clergy, but it is the disciples' job to help win and educate more disciples. Over the years I have found that I learn more about the Lord in the process of teaching others basic biblical truths. Because you are taking the time to help someone, God will expand your knowledge and intimacy with Him. The rewards are tremendous.

Step Seven: Disciple Them in the Word

In Europe, the people will often spend hours sitting around a dining table to eat, drink, and talk. They use that time to catch up with life. We can learn from them in this area of life. It offers a wonderful opportunity for sharing and for conversation about spiritual principles. The Book of Acts shows the people breaking bread together. We think of that as communion, but they saw it as a time to be together to eat, drink, and share what they learned or how the Lord moved that day.

"Disciple" means "disciplined one." It refers to being trained in a particular area of expertise. In this case, Jesus was referring to the life principles and practices He laid out.

"Because you are taking the time to help someone, God will expand your knowledge and intimacy with Him."

God loves all of us.

Jesus prayed the most amazing prayer in John 17 for us.

I do not pray for these alone, but also for those who will believe in Me through their word; that they all may be one, as You, Father, are in Me, and I in You; that they also may be one in Us, that the world may believe that You sent Me. And the glory which You gave Me I have given them, that they may be one just as We are one: I in them, and You in Me; that they may be made perfect in one, and that the world may know that You have sent Me, and have loved them as You have loved Me. (John 17:20–23)

Verse 23 focuses on the fact that the Father loves us just as much as He loves Jesus. People struggle with whether they are loved or not, but the Father loves you, me, and everyone, including those lost in sin, as much as He loves Jesus. When statements like that are made you have to ask—how much does the Father love Jesus? He loves you just as much.

"Well," some retort, "I have done all of this bad stuff." But Jesus bore it all so you would know that the Father loves you unconditionally and calls you His child.

Our God gets a lot of blame for things happening in people's lives, but as we mentioned in chapter four, the demonic realm can go unhindered through people's lives if not rebuked and run off.

He who does not love does not know God, for God is love. (I John 4:8)

The Amplified translation says it this way:

The one who does not love has not become acquainted with God [does not and never did know Him], for God is love. [He is the originator of love, and it is an enduring attribute of His nature.]

God originated unfailing love. It has always been a part of His character and makeup. The phrase "enduring attribute" means that He never changes.

Step Seven: Disciple Them in the Word

The LORD has appeared of old to me, saying: "Yes, I have loved you with an everlasting love; therefore with lovingkindness I have drawn you." (Jeremiah 31:3)

God spoke this to the children of Israel while they were steeped in idolatry and sexual perversion and about to be exiled because of their spiritual condition. The rest of Jeremiah 31 talks about restoration and the coming of the Lord to provide salvation. That is the God of love— always working to reach and restore. He is the same today.

When we talk about the love of God, I often think of Ephesians 2.

But God—so rich is He in His mercy! Because of and in order to satisfy the great and wonderful and intense love with which He loved us, even when we were dead (slain) by [our own] shortcomings and trespasses, He made us alive together in fellowship and in union with Christ; [He gave us the very life of Christ Himself, the same new life with which He quickened Him, for] it is by grace (His favor and mercy which you did not deserve) that you are saved (delivered from judgment and made partakers of Christ's salvation). (Ephesians 2:4–5 AMPC)

These two Scriptures are pregnant with revelation. God has such a wonderful and intense love for us that, even when we were dead in our sins, He made it possible for all people to be alive with Him.

Above all things have intense and unfailing love for one another, for love covers a multitude of sins [forgives and disregards the offenses of others]. (I Peter 4:8 AMPC)

Intense and unfailing love covers a multitude of sins, forgiving and disregarding the offenses of others. When I think about God's unfailing love, I often think about a mother defending her child even when they did wrong. That's an example of unfailing love. It doesn't matter what they said or did to me. I have to release the Father's intense and unfailing love to ultimately bring them into eternal life.

Jesus went through all that He did with the Father's endorsement to take sin upon Himself so we could be made the righteousness of God in Him. He loves people even if they say things about Him that are not correct. When people curse Him; when they don't give Him the time of day; or when they don't even believe He exists, He still loves them with an intense love, and He wants us to have the same compassion.

Jesus did not look at people and just say, "Poor babies." No, He had compassion. He healed and cast the devil off of them. Compassion is putting action behind your love and faith like Jesus did.

"People struggle with whether they are loved or not, but the Father loves you, me, and everyone, including those lost in sin, as much as He loves Jesus."

No matter where you are in the world, He wants us to love people with His unconditional love as we pray, intercede, and help them find their way into eternal life with the Father and

Jesus. He first died for us when no one believed. He planted the first seed of love expecting a great harvest of souls.

> *Now hope does not disappoint, because the love of God has been poured out in our hearts by the Holy Spirit who was given to us. For when we were still without strength, in due time Christ died for the ungodly. For scarcely for a righteous man will one die; yet perhaps for a good man someone would even dare to die. But God demonstrates His own love toward us, in that while we were still sinners, Christ died for us.* (Romans 5:5–8)

I have to remind myself that the love of God has been poured into my heart, and that I was once like "them."

> *But above all these things put on love, which is the bond of perfection.* (Colossians 3:14)

Or, according to the Amplified version:

> *Beyond all these things put on and wrap yourselves in [unselfish] love, which is the perfect bond of unity [for everything is bound together in agreement when each one seeks the best for others].*

To "put on" or "wrap" myself in unselfish love means that I willingly wear it like a garment. This must happen daily— sometimes many times a day as people try to knock the loving spirit right out of you. But when you wrap yourself in love and love other people, it draws people to you.

> *And we have known and believed the love that God has for us. God is love, and he who abides in love abides in God, and God in him.* (I John 4:16)

The AMPC version says it this way:

> *And we know (understand, recognize, are conscious of, by observation and by experience) and believe (adhere to and put faith in and rely on) the love God cherishes for us. God is love, and he who dwells and continues in love dwells and continues in God, and God dwells and continues in him.*

This is a great Scripture to go over and over. Even when I don't feel like it, God is love and the love of God abides in me. God cherishes us with His love. Jesus said:

> *A new commandment I give to you, that you love one another; as I have loved you, that you also love one another. By this all will know that you are My disciples, if you have love for one another.* (John 13:34–35)

It is astonishing that others will know we are His disciples when we have love for one another. All of these Scriptures really come down to this: if I want to be effective in the kingdom, then I have to put on love and remember that His love abides in me. We must demonstrate love for one another.

First Corinthians 13 tells us all the many examples of great things we can do without love, but lacking love they have no impact in the kingdom. Love is the foundation in the kingdom that causes everything to work. Yes, love never fails.

ACCOUNTABILITY

When someone is first saved, no matter how smart or how many degrees they have, the Good News refers to them as babies. Jesus delegated authority to us to help them grow spiritually. Sometimes I lose sight of how dumb I was in spiritual things when I first got saved. And yes, sometimes I still feel that way after teaching sessions where my pastor drives into infinite details to drive unbelief out. We need other believers who love Jesus around us to help steer and keep us from going off track.

At the time that I was saved, my church liked to have prophetic conferences featuring various speakers. Of course, none of them totally agreed on end-time events. I asked the pastor about it and he didn't tell me which one was correct, but what he said impacted my life in the long run: "It is important that you read and study the Word yourself. Then you will know which is the correct way."

When someone is newly saved, help them by ensuring they are growing in their relationship with the Lord. Here's a checklist to start with but feel free to add to it as the Lord leads you.

- Make sure they are plugged in to a good church. Help them get baptized.
- Meet with them periodically over coffee or other informal means to see how they're doing.
- Get them connected with a good peer group so they feel part of the whole.
- Call or text them periodically to check on them.
- Be willing to answer questions. If you don't know the answer, then help them find the answer.
- Get them plugged into groups or classes and make sure they attend.
- Help them study the Word.
- Help equip them to reach other people.

It's easy for people to wander back into their old life never to be heard from again if someone doesn't check on them periodically.

In the business world of setting scopes and planning projects, it helps to understand the purpose of the endeavor as well as inherent responsibilities and necessary skills. You need to know which resources are needed to get the job done along with timelines, budgets, and other details. The whole goal of an organization is to avoid being a one-man army trying to get everything done. The more people you have working with you in the same direction, the quicker the goals are achieved. If the expectations were not set high, then the team would never really strive for what was truly possible. It should be the same in the kingdom of God. Thank God for the apostle Paul who wrote down how the church should operate with specific offices and functions in his letter to the Ephesians.

> *Now these are the gifts Christ gave to the church: the apostles, the prophets, the evangelists, and the pastors and teachers. Their responsibility is to equip God's people to do his work and build up the church, the body of Christ. This will continue until we all come to such unity in our faith and knowledge of God's Son that we will be mature in the Lord, measuring up to the full and complete standard of Christ.* (Ephesians 4:11–13 NLT)

The apostles, prophets, evangelists, pastors, and teachers are to equip and train the people in the church on how to do His work, which includes making disciples, acts of service, and to edify and build up the church. The Amplified Bible spells out verse 12 this way:

Step Seven: Disciple Them in the Word

. . . [and He did this] to fully equip and perfect the saints (God's people) for works of service, to build up the body of Christ [the church].

As mentioned before, Jesus's ministry started with zero followers. Over time, He chose twelve apostles, training them in various acts of service, and He built them up. He taught them and gave them authority to baptize people, preach the Good News, heal the sick, and cast out demons. Then, He chose seventy more and gave them the same authority. According to I Corinthians 15:6, He was seen by over five hundred brethren at once. That's really great growth from zero followers to over five hundred in three and a half years!

In the Book of Acts, there were over one hundred twenty followers in the upper room when the Holy Spirit fell on them. In Acts 2, Peter preached the Good News and about three thousand souls were added to the church. In Acts 4, five thousand souls were added. Some of their acts of service included distribution of foods and monies, helping others, administration, church leaders, deacons, elders, and more. When I first got saved, it was not unusual to be invited to a restaurant or someone's home or business to do a Bible study. These gatherings were an immense help to me and others to get rooted in what the Bible was all about.

Typically, once someone is saved, they desire to learn and experience more. Always encourage people to attend church. Church is where relationships are established and spiritual growth occurs. Church attendance is essential for connection with others who can help. The typical church services, home groups, and Sunday schools can only go so deep, but they are a good starting point. What I didn't realize during my early beginnings was that all of this activity was discipleship. People were taking the time to teach others biblical basics. This can occur online as well as in physical locations.

Most people don't feel qualified to lead someone to the Lord or lead a Bible study. If you are plugged into a good church for a few years, I would challenge you that you know more than 95 percent of the people in the world. Besides, preparing for a Bible study lesson causes you to study more. The one teaching gets more out of it than the students! It also causes you to listen to your pastor more closely for material. There are times when I ask the Lord to have my pastor address a certain issue while preaching. The Lord is faithful. If you ask Him for information, He will provide it. Challenge yourself and others to train others for works of service. It takes practice, and over time you will get stronger and feel better about it.

As you are walking, driving, or perhaps flying, take the time to see the people. Ask the Lord about them. Ask if He wants you to go start a conversation and ultimately see if there is something the Lord wants you to pray with them about. Who knows? You may be impacting their eternal destination.

To read more on conversing about Jesus, I recommend the book *How to Talk about Jesus without Freaking Out: Sharing Your Faith through Three Compelling Stories*, by Victorya Michaels Rogers.

"It's easy for people to wander back into their old life never to be heard from again if someone doesn't check on them periodically."

Step Seven: Disciple Them in the Word

WISDOM FROM VICKI

I try to find common ground with people. It may start with a compliment on something they are wearing, how they handle themselves, or life experiences we have in common—children, grandchildren, parents, troubles, economy, whatever.

If someone is visibly hurting physically or emotionally, be kind and compassionate. Ask them if you can pray for them right there. After praying, I ask whether they go to church. If they do not attend anywhere, I give them suggestions.

When I am in the office, I sit with my Bible or another Christian book open. This will often draw comments of praise from saved people but will also draw questions from others. The open Bible on the desk is one way to get a conversation started.

When I'm speaking with someone I don't know, I try to bring God into each conversation somehow. Again, I may ask, "What church do you go to?" This gives me some idea of where they are spiritually. If I hear a convicted comment, then I try to probe further to see why they feel convicted. The Lord gives you words to say as you go.

Depending on their responses, I may ask, "Can you give God a good reason why He would allow you into heaven?" Also, I may ask them, "If you died today, do you know if you would go to heaven?"

Act interested and see where the discussion goes. Don't be offended if they don't want to speak. They may not be ready yet but offer to keep them in prayer.

A few years ago, I asked the Lord if He would like me to mentor (disciple) someone. I just had a desire to do this. Within one month, I had four ladies reach out to me asking to be mentored. All of them needed help. Many times, we just have to be willing to invest the time. The Lord will open doors of opportunities. It just takes commitment and faithfulness to see people through from their current situation to receiving the Lord until they elevate up to impacting their church and community. Usually after praying with people to receive the Lord, I will stress the importance of taking this seriously. Be committed and faithful to Him all the days of your life. God is looking for committed Christians.

Chapter 11

Sample Prayers for Salvation and Rededication

I t is essential for the person you are leading to the Lord or who is rededicating their life to say what you say. The challenge is not the words but getting them to open their mouth and say it.

> *The Father loves the Son, and has given all things into His hand. He who believes in the Son has everlasting life; and he who does not believe the Son shall not see life, but the wrath of God abides on him.* (John 3:35–36)

Some people choose to go down what is called the "Romans Road" to start the process, which includes:

- Romans 3:23 says that all have sinned and fallen short of the glory of God.
- Romans 5:8 says that even when we were still sinners Christ died for us.

- Romans 10:13 says that all of those who call on the name of the Lord will be saved.

If you openly declare that Jesus is Lord and believe in your heart that God raised him from the dead, you will be saved. For it is by believing in your heart that you are made right with God, and it is by openly declaring your faith that you are saved. (Romans 10:9–10 NLT)

SAMPLE PRAYER OF SALVATION

Heavenly Father, in Jesus's name, I ask You to forgive my sins. I am sorry for denying You all these years. I openly declare that Jesus is Lord. I believe in my heart that You died for me and that God raised Jesus from the dead. Because I believe in my heart, I am made right with God. I choose to live and serve You all the days of my life as my Lord and Savior. I openly declare by faith I am now saved!

SAMPLE PRAYER REDEDICATING PEOPLE TO THE LORD

Heavenly Father, in Jesus's name, I come to You in repentance to confess my sins to You and ask You to help me overcome _____, which has been leading me away from You. I rededicate my life to You and trust in You. Thank You for Your great mercy and love and that my life is renewed in You. I will serve You all the days of my life as Lord and Savior, in Jesus's name!

Appendix 1

Summary Prayers and Sayings

BIND THE ENEMY OFF OF THEIR MINDS

ather, in the name of Jesus, You have given us authority to tread on scorpions and serpents and over all the power of the enemy. I come against the devil that is blinding the eyes of _____ and I command him off of _____ so he or she has the opportunity to hear the Good News. Devil, you can't stop this person from being saved in Jesus's name.

If you are praying for someone who has lost a loved one, it is far more effective for <u>the individual</u> to speak this than for us to speak it on their behalf. It is good training to deal with demonic attacks in their lives or the lives of people they come into contact with.

Prayer for Jewish People to Be Saved

Father, in the name of Jesus, I ask that You take the blinders off of the eyes of the Jewish people who have not yet accepted You. However You need to—do it. Cause dreams, witnesses, and other means. Cause them to come to the knowledge of the truth that Jesus is their Lord and Savior. We rebuke the tradition and stubbornness that will keep them from seeking You out. You told them early on that if they seek You, You will be found. In Jesus's name, hearts be open to the truth of Jesus.

Prayer to Loose the Holy Spirit into Their Life

Couple this with the prayer above on binding the enemy off of them.

Father, in the name of Jesus, I loose the Holy Spirit into _____ life, to convict them of the sin of not knowing Jesus as their Lord and Savior. I give the Holy Spirit free rein in their life to do whatever it takes to bring them into the knowledge of You in Jesus's name.

Prayer to Send Laborers into Their Life

Father, in Jesus's name, I know You desire all people to be saved and come to knowledge of the truth. Concerning _____, I pray in accordance with Your Word that You send laborers across their path to ultimately bring them into relationship with You. I also call upon the angels to work in conjunction with laborers who've been chosen and picked out for _____.

Summary Prayers and Sayings

Let Your laborers be in the right place at the right time with the right words to say. In Jesus's name, I give You permission to do what it takes to lead them into acceptance of Jesus as their Lord and Savior.

I always like to add, "Do what it takes to bring them in," because some people are more stubborn than others. You are giving the Lord and the angels permission to do whatever it takes, meaning, "Don't leave them alone until they accept You as Lord and Savior!"

PRAYER TO OPEN THEIR HEART TO HEAR

Father, in Jesus's name, I ask that, by the power of the Holy Spirit, You open up _____ heart to the Good News being preached, no matter what the method. Along with laborers I command all channels of hearing to be activated so that they hear and come into the knowledge of the truth.

SPEECH TO KEEP IN LINE WITH YOUR PRAYER

Isaiah 54:13 – All my children are taught by the Lord and great shall be the peace of my children.

I Timothy 2:4 – My desire and prayer is that _____ is saved and comes to the knowledge of the truth.

Acts 11:14 – My desire is for _____ to receive the words by which they and all their household will be saved.

For the Jewish person:

Romans 9:27 – Though the number of the children of Israel be as the sand of the sea, the remnant _____ are saved.

Praises That Align with What Has Been Prayed

Lord, I praise You that You desire none be lost but all come into the saving knowledge of You.

Lord, I praise You that _____ is saved.

Lord, I praise You that _____ is serving You and reaching other people for the kingdom of God.

Lord, I praise You that my children are taught of the Lord and great is their peace.

Lord, I praise You that the seed of the righteous shall be delivered.

Prayer of Salvation

Heavenly Father, in Jesus's name, I ask You to forgive my sins. I am sorry for denying You all these years. I openly declare that Jesus is Lord. I believe in my heart that You died for me and that God raised Jesus from the dead. Because I believe in my heart, I am made right with God. I choose to live and serve You all the days of my life as my Lord and Savior. I openly declare by faith I am now saved!

Summary Prayers and Sayings

PRAYER OF REDEDICATION

Heavenly Father, in Jesus's name, I come to You in repentance to confess my sins to You and ask You to help me overcome _____, which has been leading me away from You. I re-dedicate my life to You and trust in You. Thank You for Your great mercy and love and that my life is renewed in You. I will serve You all the days of my life as Lord and Savior, in Jesus's name!

Appendix 2

Prayer Journal

The demonic realm loves to get us off track, keep us super busy, or bring pressure and attacks from multiple directions. The Lord loves when someone takes the time to pray what is in His heart. The prayer journal we've included in the following pages is intended to help you record and track people and prayers over time as you follow the seven steps outlined in this book. It always helps me to write down who I'm praying for, the date I started, and insights from the Lord during the process, including when they accepted Jesus as their Lord and Savior.

You'll notice we labeled the left side "Name or Group." People groups, for example, can be various neighborhoods, religious groups who don't believe in Jesus, your family, and countries.

I keep a growing list of people as the Lord brings others to my thoughts so I can more easily circle back and cover each person. You can also celebrate as you return to your list and record not only prayers sent up, but prayers answered!

Name or Group	Notes

Prayer Journal

Name or Group   Notes

_____   _____

_____   _____

_____   _____

_____   _____

_____   _____

_____   _____

_____   _____

_____   _____

_____   _____

_____   _____

_____   _____

_____   _____

_____   _____

_____   _____

_____   _____

_____   _____

Name or Group	Notes
_____	_____
_____	_____
_____	_____
_____	_____
_____	_____
_____	_____
_____	_____
_____	_____
_____	_____
_____	_____
_____	_____
_____	_____
_____	_____
_____	_____
_____	_____
_____	_____

Prayer Journal

Name or Group	Notes

SEE *the* PEOPLE

Name or Group   Notes

_____   _____

_____   _____

_____   _____

_____   _____

_____   _____

_____   _____

_____   _____

_____   _____

_____   _____

_____   _____

_____   _____

_____   _____

_____   _____

_____   _____

_____   _____

_____   _____

_____   _____

_____   _____

_____   _____

_____   _____

_____   _____

_____   _____

_____   _____

Dear Friends

I hope you enjoyed **SEE tHE PEOPLE**. If you were inspired by the book, we invite you to ask your friends and relatives to read it as well.

Here are a few ways that you can help us spread the word:

- Recommend the book to friends – word-of-mouth is still the most effective form of advertising.
- Purchase additional copies to give away as gifts on my website.
- Post a 5-Star review on Amazon.
- Write about the book on your Facebook, X, Instagram, LinkedIn—any social media you use!
- If you blog, consider referencing the book, or publishing an excerpt from the book with a link back to my website. You have my permission to do this if you provide proper credit and backlinks.